One hand cannot clap...
     Ga proverb

'Tis courtesy, not necessity, counsels the hen to genuflect when crossing a threshold
     Ga proverb

This Adinkra symbol is called Agye Nyame – except God – traditionally symbolizes the recognition of the omnipotence of God

MANDELA
THE SPEAR
AND OTHER POEMS

· P U B L I S H I N G ·

First published 2008 by the Publishing Division of the Ghana
Publishing Company Ltd. Assembly Press, Accra, Ghana

This 2013 edition...

African Perspectives Publishing

PO Box 95342
Grant Park 2051
South Africa

Email: francis@africanperspectives.co.za

www.africanperspectives.co.za

ISBN 978-0-9921875-1-4

Edited by Fred Odametey

Typeset by Gail Day

Cover design by Future Brand
from the Nelson Mandela Capture Site designed by
Marco Cianfanelli and photographed by Jonathan Burton –
themidlandsphotographer.weekly.com

Printed and bound by 4 Colour Print

DEDICATION

**to
Osagyefo Dr. Kwame Nkrumah
and the masses of
the United States of Africa**

DEDICATION
to

Kofi Okwabi / Ago Kuma / Ayorkor Kuma / Pauline Clark /
Eva Korsah / Theresa Bekoe / E. Evans-Anfom / Nii Amon
Kotei / K. K. Korsah / J. E. Allotey-Pappoe / Diane Stephenson
/ Ronald Van Orden / Iris Torto / Christian Aggrey / Nii Anum
Telfer / Orlando Marville / Paa C. Oshipi Quaye / Abi George /
Setheli Ashong-Katai / Angelita Reyes / Kobena Eyi Acquah /
Raymond Akwule / Nee Djan Dodoo / Estella Sales / Jawa
Apronti / Aki Sawyerr / Kwesi Botchway / Willie Amarfio /
E. J. Thompson / Jacob Ofori Ashong / K. A. Bilson /
J. T. Nartey / John Kwabena Mensah / Edmond Ekuban /
Daniel Odonkor / E. C. Quaye / Robert Manning / Laurent
J. M. Diatta / V. V. Hutchison / Evelyn Amarteifio / Akua
Asaabea / Henry Quist / Nana Odei Ofei / Ajoa Yeboah-Afari /
Gausu Diawarra / Gelli Abdul Rahman / Bob Cobbing / Jeni
Cozeyn / George McBeth / D. A. Nii Amponsah / Abraham
Arthur / Diana Maynel / Nana Kwasi Asante-Sakyi / James
Millar / Oforiwa Mate / Henri Swanzy / Elizabeth Sackey /
Willie Donkor / Geraldine Fiawoo / Safoa Ayerh / Evans
Hunter / F. S. K. Owusu / E. M. Lamptey / D. Lomgo / J. Manful
/ Gladys Mensah / W. Ofosuhene / J. W. Okai / I. K. Okpoti /
Elizabeth Olletey / E. M. Opoku / A. Osibey / J. K. Forkuoh /
B. O. Gbeve / G. M. Gyekye / J. E. Haizel / R. M. Hammond /
C. L. Hesse / R. Koranteng / Merley Korley / B. K. Kporvie /
A. Kumah / J. Kusi-Appiah / T. K. Kwame / Mabel Atiegar /
G. Awadey / P. Awuah / P. A. Bannerman / T. Bortey /
A. M. Commey / I. Damoah / F. Darko / S. K. Darku / B. Djan /
F. Doku-Dolley / T. N. Dowuona / A. J. Abanyie / E. M. Abudu /
W. O. Adofo / E. Agyepong / S. Ahene / J. L. Akrong /
C. Ammah / N. A. Ammah / Constance Anang / E. B. Anang /
E. O. Ankrah / D. Ansger / D. Anum / J. Aryee / K. S. Aryee /
E. M. Peprah / H. Quarshie / J. Q. Quartey / E. A. Sackey /
D. Sowah / B. Sulley / G. Tawiah / Teye / I. K. Vanderpuije

CONTENTS

FOREWORD

It is, I must admit, a special and generous mark of honour to be offered the chance to write a Preface to this latest collection of Okai's poetry. For indeed, neither the poems, nor Okai himself, need my voice – the poet has long established himself as one of the towering figures in the field of modern African poetry in English.

He is one of the pioneers who, taking off from the legacy of predecessors like Christopher Okigbo, Kofi Awoonor and Aimé Césaire – themselves heirs of the Harlem Renaissance – launched in the second half of the last century into a vigorous reinvention of the poetic genre, aiming through an iconoclastic, if not exuberant, approach to lexis, syntax and phonology, to create a poetry that would be close both to orality and to our indigenous folk traditions.

These new poets were men of great linguistic ingenuity. They assembled words surrealistically, in a bold and adventurous game of bricolage, forcing meaning not so much from the words' familiar semantic connotations, but rather from their sounds, from the startling shock (or unexpected harmony) of colliding vowels and consonants, the astonishing but brilliant felicity forced out of unusual lexical weldings and phrasal alliances, or by the erratic relocation (or erasure) of punctuations.

Then, in addition to this deliberate, chaotic approach to grammar and graphology, the poets also exercised, in varying degrees of inspired eccentricity, a wanton spirit of linguistic hybridity, transiting at will from one language to another in the same poem or even the same verse, all in an attempt to tame the "strangeness" of English with the jargon of local words, phrases, idiomatic expressions, and proverbs.

These experimentations have led, in the best of these poets, to astoundingly beautiful and powerful works – and Okai has always been among the best, in that select list which includes Kofi Anyidoho, Niyi Osundare, and Tanure Ojaide.

Rapidly therefore they stamped their authority on the literary world in Africa and on the international circuit, with both their innovative techniques and aggressive political advocacy. They revolutionized the poet/audience relationship, changed the mode of expression from mere scriptography to narratology, and the role of the audience from that of passive reception to active participation. Performance became the preferred medium of delivery; the communal experience and destiny, rather than the individual angst, replaced the creative impulse. Okai and his contemporaries thus created a new poetic paradigm that has remained unsurpassed for decades now, for all the controversy it has generated and continues to generate.

II

From his very first collection, entitled Flowerfall, (1969), to the second, The Oath of The Fontomfrom and Other Poems (1971), and the last, Lorgorligi Logarithms and Other Poems (1988), Okai established a very powerful presence as an oral performer, whose readings galvanized audiences across the world, from Accra to Abuja, Tema to Tripoli, Legon to Lagos, Dakar to Dar es Salaam, Cairo to Khartoum, Monrovia, Nairobi, Moscow, New York, Los Angeles, and several other places.

And then, mysteriously, at the very summit of this acclamation, when his work was garnering prestigious awards, Okai retreated abruptly into a baffling silence. He had chosen, it seemed, to shift his focus to purely administrative duties, in his new position as the Secretary General of the PAWA, to which he was elected in 1990.

But now, thankfully, that interlude of drought is over at last, and the appearance of this new collection will certainly gladden many of us who are his admirers. It consists of a number of new, as well as some old, poems and show that Okai is not only still waxing as strong as ever, but that also, in many delectable instances, he has grown mellow, stronger and more assured.

Listen to him, for instance in the third sequence of "The Bond Oath of Ubuntu":

> I am the soul.
> I am the goal.
> I am the footprint of man.
> I am the heart. I am the hope.
> I am the ancestral horoscope.
> I am the pathfinder's map.
> (...)
> I am the light. I am the future.
> I am that I am.
>
> I AM UBUNTU...
> I AM UBUNTU...
>
> I AM AFRICA!

Readers will find that all the familiar elements of the Okai signature are present here, in this new offering – the declamatory posture of the poet- persona; the tactical deployment of assonances and alliterations, of anaphora, onomatopoeia and ideophone to create an aural effect; a polyglot jouissance in lexical choice; the mobilization of memory and remembrance for cultural propaganda; the constant mingling of customary codes and the violent conjoining of names from diverse epochs and places, as practised in ritual conjuration, etc – all these and more are patently in evidence here.

The strength of the Okai poem – a fact very vital to any useful interpretation of it – is in its conception, not as sustained narrative or philosophical meditation, but rather, as panegyric, or thaumaturgic utterance, or ritual prayer. This is why it tends to rely, much like in our sacred dramas, far more on the power of sheer pronouncement, of direct evocation, more than on elaborate tropes.

One can almost say that for Okai, as for some of his contemporaries, merely to speak, to pronounce, is to bring into being. Hence this obvious predilection for incantative methods and sonorous invocations, the recourse to the sorcery of sound effects, to words and phrases with percussive suggestions.

This is to say therefore that the poems are mostly re-configured praise-poems, tributes to out- standing heroes, and to significant landmarks and events in the black and African history.

It is this burning desire to celebrate the black experience and culture, through the iconic figures who symbolize our struggles and triumphs, that governs the collection. Thus, not surprisingly, we encounter names like Mandela, Nadine Gordimer, Amilcar Cabral, Patrice Lumumba, Kwame Nkrumah, and so on. Achievement is the measure of choice, and Okai does not discriminate – alongside these political stalwarts feature successful artistes and even football stars: all that matters is that we should emulate them and like them, change our world:

Ousmane Sembene and
Kwesi Owusu, change the
Guard, the ocean is not the same.
Consult the contour map of the soul.
Alter geography. Rearrange the sky.

THE EAGLE WILL FLY

Kwaw Ansah and Ngugi
Wa Thiong'o, rearrange the images.
Change the direction of the wind.
Guide her feet to the hill.
Subpoena the gods.

THE EAGLE WILL FLY...
['A Concerto for Black Satellites']

Okai's agenda seeks to recruit all of us into the army of
people like Cabral, whom he claims to have seen

Destabilizing bridges,
Tendering flowers,
Whispering certain addresses
Into the ears
Of the gathering tongues of fire

And leading cattle to pastures and springs
And singing songs that summon sounds
That pour pails of pure well-water
Unto the tired spirit.
['Fanfare for Cabral']

Most of the time, Okai's message gushes along in form of
allusion and suggestion. However, occasionally, he is moved
to be blunt in his anger, as in the poem "Fanfare for Cabral"

where he arranges the familiar lyrics of a kindergarten song into a chant of race-retrieving menace:

> See me Lakayana with my spear –
> The spear which my grandfather gave me,
> My grandfather who fought the Whiteman,
> The Whiteman who stole our lands,
> The Whiteman who thinks he's here for ever.
>
> See me Lakayana with my spear –
> The beautiful ones are now being born. ...
>
> SEE ME LIKE A HYENA IN YOUR FEARS.
>   ['Fanfare for Cabral']

In another sequence of another long poem, written under the influence of Sunny Okosuns, and in a gesture reminiscent of Osundare and Ojaide, Okai plunges angrily into direct indictment of the local exploiters:

> ...The gods of Agege cannot ignore
>
> that it was God who created the human jaw
> in both the man with the Swiss bank account
> and the beggar chanting by the rich door...
> (....)
>
> who owns the land and who owns the gold?
> who tills the land and who eats the yam?
> (....)
>
> who owns the land and who sells the cocoa?
> who tills the land and who eats the corn?
>
> who owns the land and who sells the timber?
> who mans the land and who mans the borders?...
>   ['And Now to End the World News']

But still, such instances of raw fury are few. There are also gentle moments, subtle recollections; and the collection does bring us at least one love poem ("Still Life: Lily Lawns…"), where the poet speaks with surprising tenderness:

> to say that you are
> beautiful, though,
>
> is to say
> that in winter snow falls.
>
> and yesterday
> I would have said the same
> about the clay
> and about all things that claim
> a name…

But it is the concluding lines of the poem, (which are also those of the collection), that are especially felicitous. Like those of a possessed prophet on the mystic mountain, Okai's words bring us intimations of a coming benediction, of epiphany:

> And the happy horizon again is aflame
> with the timid light of rebirth,
> the darkness again is departing
> like a lover withdrawing at dawn
> to the cricket's concerto
> and the tadpole's tattoo.
>
> The mist of morning is milky in the air,
> the honey of hope is high in the head,
> the bonfires of faith are frolicking into force…."

And it is from this rapturous vision then that the poet is able to end his journey on the promise of redemption, glory and grace:

> I see him. I can see him now.
> I have caught him at it.
> He is doing it again.
>
> > GOD AGAIN IS SPRINKLING
> > THINGS
> > ALL OVER THE PLACE
>
> The gold of the soul, the jewels
> > of the spirit,
> the diamonds of the mind,
> > the pearls of labouring hands,
> the precious minerals of the
> > earth
> and the bounteous fruits
> > of the fields...
> showers of blessings upon us.
>
> The morning marigolds gather again
> In the mountain gardens of Gethsemane.
> The midnight glories flower afresh
> In the dawn time fanfare for fairies.
>
> Amen.

Amen for Okai. Amen for this collection. Amen for all of us.

FEMI OSOFISAN
February 2007
Ibadan

ATUKWEI OKAI

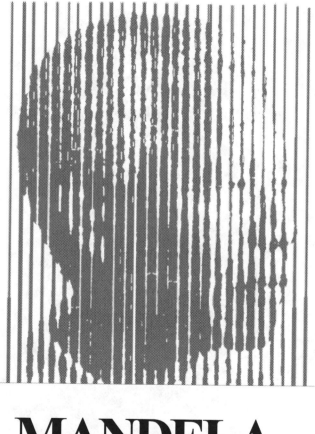

MANDELA
THE SPEAR
AND **OTHER POEMS**

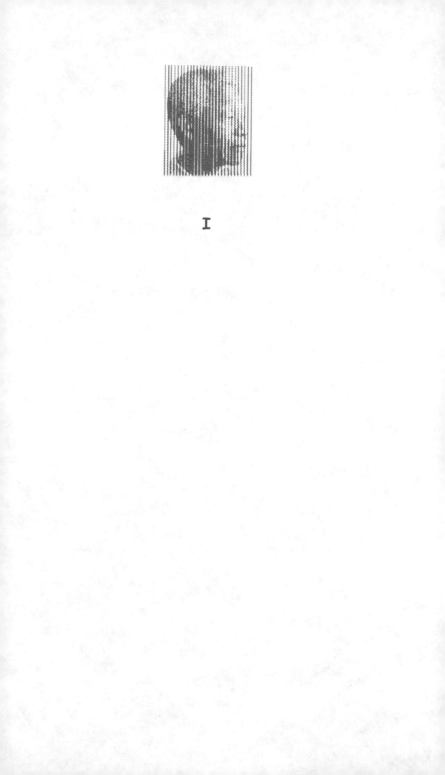

I

THE ROSETTA STONE
IN THE MEANTIME OF ETERNITY

dedicated with love to the African people,
the founding fathers of the OAU and
Madam Fathia Nkrumah

It is like a dream. I am in Egypt.

From ancient Alexandria's Pompeii's
Pillar,
From Gamel Abdel Nassar's Cairo
Tower,
Together with Sando Anoff, I do not
Cower
Before the cold force of winds
    blowing with furious Pharaonic power
As we quest around like Samouri and Babatou
    to see enough
As Cairo,
    in glittering bits and sombre pieces,
Sprawls around like a horizontalized
    anthill.

Peering across over the exposed heads
    of eel-like cars, reeling skyscrapers,
    innocent hats, huts and spaces,

I look, like a latter-day native Napoleon
Bonaparte (he, after all, did not hail
    from these parts)

And see enough of the patiently proud
And eternally prayerful pyramids
(take away the crowd, take away the shroud,)

At Saharan solitude's Sakkara,

And the God-gazing time-testing eternal
Trinity
Of the triple nipples

Of the pyramids upon the sun-saluting
Sphinx-plateau at Giza,

PYRAMIDS PERPERTUALLY PERCHED

In the prayerful meantime of elusive
Eternity
Upon the invisible steadfast
Architectural
Pebbles

Of humanity's first and eternally
Anonymous
Super-Pythagoras.

Out of history's and distance's concealing
Mist,

The pyramidal parabola conjures forth
Our Table Mountain in her fire-necklaced,
    bullet-spitting, fire-fractured
South
Where zealous Azania, like a provoked

Chaka the Zulu,

Is in wrath, since at the Cape of Good but
Useless Hope,
The water of life has been rendered
Poisonous and rough.

Sanity's horizon is hanging on a rope.
Towards her, sleepwalkers stagger and grope

As if on dope.

From the Cairo Tower,
    give me a Jeff Asmah helicopter view
    of things -
I AM SEARCHING FOR OUR ROSETTA STONE.

We must find out for what and what
We must atone.
With Cheik Anta Diop and Brother Boutrous
Boutrous-Ghali
We journey from ancient Songhai to medieval
Mali.

I see
   the fortress-temple of Muhammad Ali,
I see the lotus flower perfume
The Anyidoho-Dey
   ever-dawning centuries
In the lullaby midnight alabaster limbs
   of the belly dancer Souher Zaki.

I see the Zimbabwe Ruins, Thomas Sankara,

And the Victoria Falls
   and their sentinels,
Jumoke, Rosemarie Anoff and Farouk Hosni,

Drink in the sounds of the city
   of a thousand minarets that mine
   the minds of worlds that should not be
   at rest.

I see the life-giving Nile and the city
   of the dead (and who says they

   and dead!),
In the largest city on medieval earth,
   Cairo,
   I see the University-mosque of Al-Azhar;
her doors are ajar.

Rock-carrying ass, sled-drawing ox,
Chisel and mattock,

Princely seducers of immortality -
The majestic
   bas-relief seek to give relief

To the mortality marooned, like the sun
    in the galaxy, in the air
    we breathe.

We must break the code
    of the Rosetta Stone
To decipher
The hieroglyphics of our destiny.

IN THIS CRUSADE, ARE WE ALONE?

Ancestors Nkrumah and Nassar,
    we hear your voices sounding
From afar -
We see you on horses, you the spirit
    of our forces.

The thunder today carries the clear
Voice-print of Kwame and Gamal.
The coded message activates the preemptive
Strike
Of Tutankhamen's jackal.

The sunrise today
    Bears
    the clear fingerpirnt of Akhenaton.

EGYPT IS ONE. AFRICA IS ONE.
GOD IS ONE.
    La illa illala!

Upon the shifting forehead of Cairo's
Golden sands,
I read the hieroglyphics of time
    and my heart understands:

IN THE MEANTIME OF ETERNITY

Discover the key
    that breaks the code
Of the oracle of our destiny.

THE BOND-OATH OF UBUNTU

to Salim Ahmed Salim

I

"The Number You Are Calling Is
    Not In Service At This Time ...
The Number You Are Calling Is
    Not In Service At This Time ..."

DON'T YOU GIVE ME THAT JAZZ!

I know
There are people at the other end.
Don't ask
My dreams to convey contraband
Cargoes
Into the saharas of some unlisted
Mongolia.

O
I can clearly hear my very beginnings
Humming like
A Papua New Guinea peacock
On heat
In the archipelagos of the ages.
I must excavate in me the embargoed
Plateau zones of our vision-friendly
Utopia:
The legend of the Battle of Adowa:
The song, the totem, and the assegai.

Within the silently seething, digitized
Intestines of prehistoric Tanzania,
My soul's cosmic umbilical cord,
Like a blanket-clad stone-age refugee

Anticipating a passport and a visa,
Awaits the connection with Ethiopia,
With Alexandria.

I must link myself with another -
I must link myself with another -
Within
The oasis-compound of the
Awakened.

II

The Lalibela Temple
Stands sentry
Over the shimmering threshold
Of the twenty-first century.

The millennium new
Calculates
The Timbuktooyan-Tutankhammenic
Spirito-stratospheric physics
Of her majestic entry.

Upon the Table Mountain,
Inscribe on
The other side of the Rosetta Stone

The classified spiritual inventory
Of man, woman
And humanity ...

III

Out of the moon-massaging mouth
Of the monumental midnight

Mmenson of Marrakesh
And the longlong Sokoto-Sudanese
Horns of Sojourner Truth,
Rivalling the eternity-teasing
Nefertiti neck,

From within the savannah-seducing,
Anthill-saluting vocal chords
Of the Kalahari xylophone,
From within the colanut-custodian
Calabash of the kora
Of Mount Kilimanjaro,
From inside the forest diviner
Depths
Of the Obintin Obonu drums of
Mantse Tackie Tawia
And Chaka the Zulu,
And the balafong
Of the Futajalon and River Congo,

The earth of Fianarantsoa pours
Out

The wind of the stone citadel
Of the Great Zimbabwe pours
OUT
The fire of Monomotapa pours
OUT

Through the gurgling
Pharaonic, fontomfromic, wailing
Waters
Of the Victoria Falls,
    Abu Simbel
       And Akosombo,

THE TRANSCENDENTAL
   ABYSSINIA-TANZANIA
      CRADLE CHORUS-ANTHEM:

I testify to the coconut's sap,
I notify of the landmine and
The gap.

I am the soul. I am the goal.
I am the footprint of man.
I am the heart. I am the hope.
I am the ancestral horoscope.
I am the pathfinder's map.

I am the bloodprint of the air.
I am the soulprint of the sun.

I am the blueprint of the gene.
I am the umbilical cord
TO MANKIND.

I am the compass finger
TO THE MILLENNIUM -

I AM THE
FOOTPRINT OF THE WORLD.

I am the light.
I am the future.
I am that I am.

I AM UBUNTU . . .
I AM UBUNTU . . .

I AM AFRICA !

STILL LIFE: LILLY LAWNS...
LITTLE LEGON... MOONLIGHT BALLET

to Olly Davy-Hayford

this girl's face looks familiar
her hair spells the scent bougainvillea

in the midst of a wood near Macedonia.

I pawn memories to feelings
perpendicular.

to ask you to smile I hope
is not to ask the moon
to dance by day.

to say that you are
beautiful, though,

is to say
that in winter snow falls.

and yesterday
I would have said the same
about the clay
and about all things that claim
a name.

I would have said
the trees grow in my garden
sending their roots downwards.

by the light of a candleflame
I search for you amidst
the blind wind
of a rainy night.

A CONCERTO FOR THE BLACK SATELLITES:
IN THE STOOLROOM OF THE SOUL

to Kwesi Botchway, Aki Sawyerr
and Nana Danso Abiam

I

Joern Utzon
made his spiritual point
decades ago
    at Bennelong Point.
He would sleep
    with both eyes open,
as wide open
    as the three hundred
feet his vision poured
    into the most
democratic staircase
    on planet earth,
an open embrace
    for all the truth
and fairplay
    that the Noah's Ark
could hold
    that came walking upon
the waters
from England's receding shores.

II

Utzon slices up

Osam Duodo's spherical ball
Into the orange peel shapes
    to mould
Sail-shell roofs
    for the beauty
Of unattainable truth
In his celestial
    Sydney Opera house.

III

Together
With Baba Yara and Mohammed Ali,
I am there
In your Kwame Saarah-Mensah knees,
Banini and Dan Addo; dribble, fly
Like a leap-year zebra in the green
Turf jungles of the amazing
Saturday Amazon-Congo.

"Moro-Moro...

The Moroccan wizard sleeps
With one eye open."
As long Azumah Nelson shots
Scatter the field, Ofei Dodoo is

There in your Otto Pfister toes
Which have paid their dues, Duah
And Arhinful; seduce the ball

Into a forty-five degree whirl
Like a fire-eating snake-charmer
In the Mantse Agbonaa playing
Fields

Of timeless Timbuktoo.

"Moro-Moro...

The Moroccan wizard
Sleeps
With one eye open."

Kuffour and Akunnor conceive and
Command the Saka-Saka park
Corner kick onto the Roger Milla
Unturbaned heads

Of Asare and Asare;
In the century's own sacred
Saturday safari, the stadium
Burts
Its hydro-electric human banks,
Splashing multi-billion drops
Of baptismal/confirmatory
Holy water
Into the thirsty spiritual eyes
Of the doubting thomases

Of mankind.

Moro-Moro...

Oldman Omar Mukhtarr and Amarkai
Are there in your Osam Duodu
Fingers, goalguard Ben Owu;
Jump and stretch out like
A giraffe. Embosom

The pythenoid horizon-gulping
Fireball like
A Kintampo-Sydney Cove kangaroo.

The designer passes of assegai-
Darting Nii Odartey Lamptey,
Soccerdom's
Magical, jujucal Picasso,

Like monsoon time aladdin lamps
In the hanging gardens of the mind,
Neutralise the panga poisin
In the counter kick of the

Boomerangoid ballistic ball.

The Odartey Lamptey cheetah
Chess move

Moves all my Mohammed Gargo
Mountains,

In the name of Mohammed

— GOD IS THE GREATEST.

The odyssey of your Naa Dzeringa
Borderguard dribbling legs do not
Leave my spirits in the lurch,
Mohammed Gargo. Gargo charges
Against the
Goalkeeper's citadel fortress
Like a Limpopo River leopard.

"Moro-Moro...

The Moroccan wizard
Sleeps
With one eye
Open."

IV

CREATION DAY IS HERE AGAIN

Bareheaded, bare-chested Oduduwa,
I walk the Ile-Ife Zimbabwe
Ruins in the rain.

Justine Naana Mensah, and
Gaston Kabore, just adjust
The camera, change the lenses,
Audition the cast, rewrite the
Script.

THE EAGLE WILL FLY

Osman Sembene and
Kwesi Owusu, change the
Guard, the ocean is not the same.
Consult the contour map of the soul.
Alter geography. Rearrange the sky.

THE EAGLE WILL FLY

Kwaw Ansah and Ngugi
Wa Thiong'o, rearrange the images,
Change the direction of the wind.
Guide her feet to the hill.
Subpoena the gods.

THE EAGLE WILL FLY

Kwaate Nii Owoo,
We are out of the woods, intone
Your mama's warning words:

"Moro-Moro..."

In the stool room of the soul,
The returning officer reads out
The name on the ballot papers:

Gaston
Gaston Kabore
Gaston Kabore
Kabore Gaston

Kabore
Kabore
Gaston Kabore.

THE EAGLE WILL FLY

V

The referee plants
His soothsayer whistle
Between his
Unquivering judicial Turkish
Lips,
And again into the
King Tackie Kome-Okomfo Anokye
African sky,

Like an Akosombo-Ouagadougou
Commando Masai,
A rapid deployment force of
Black satellites
Into the unfettered firmament,
Like Kwegyir Aggrey's eagle,
Leaps.

And the soul,
Away from her bastion of faith,

Sweeps
The lingering dust of doubts,

Summoning
The long-silenced Sokoto long

Horns to shout:
>   by transcendental helicopter
>   the dream has landed.
>   let us go into a forest retreat
>   for we must fast.
>   into the twenty-first century
>   we emerge from the past.
>   the ancestors take a look,
>   they are no longer aghast.
>   in the stoolroom of the soul,
>   the die is cast.

VI

In the stoolroom of the soul,
The African dream scores her goal.

Across
The sands of sun-saturated Sahara
As far as where the sea horizons
With the sky in an eternal embrace,

The palanquins of the people's
Passion
Bear your crowns of genius and
Honour.

The ancestors bless the
Generational feat,
The Utzon-Osam Duoduan drums
Repeat:

AGAINST

All cancerous
Canker of broad daylight deceit,
Like the rose water-sipping,
     Topaz-tinted, man-carved

Sydney Opera House,

OUR SOUL IS ON SEAT . . .
OUR SOUL IS ON SEAT . . .

AND THE EAGLE HAS FLOWN!

II

THE GUILLOTINE OF TIME:
FANFARE FOR THE UNCOMMON WOMAN

for NADINE GORDIMER AT 75

AARON COPELAND -

How are we to cope with the land?

PABLO PICASSO -

Who is there to declare what is not so?
How are we to tell where we must go?
Where are we to stop to relate our woe?

GEORGE GERSHWIN -

Wrap the sordid song in a magical mauve,
Get the whirlwind to whip the whispers
In the grove.

May our Sontonga rhapsody soar
In Abdullah Ibrahim, Miriam Makeba
And Hugh Masekela.

(II)

Harvest across the land

The fresh George Bizos asparagus.
Summon into the museum
The Walter Chakela charitable chariot.
Crumble down
The Arthur Molepo chastising chalice.
Quarantine in dust

The Tina Mnumzana bedroom bellows.
Decentralize
The Nkotsi Sol Plaatije soul's solitude.

Scatter over the land
The Gerard Sekoto quota of blues and pink,

And pink, greens and red.

I HEAR THE CHIMES OF SANITY
IN THE UNHURRIED GUILLOTINE
OF TIME.

(III)

In the jacaranda month
        of sunlight-spangled November,
Where and how - only
        the ocean depths can remember -
Conception occurs of the soul
        deemed for Nadine Gordimer.
Clear as spring water rising from
        the depths of the benevolent
        earth,
The graffiti from the wilderness
        of her soul, since birth,
Spring into the skies over
        the valley of a thousand hills -

(They read like the classified details
of her multiple wills!)

Jacaranda petals, daytime diamonds
        of the jazzy Johannesburg skies,
Dangle a necklace of prophecies
In front of her radar-like soul-reading
        Eyes

Within which her baffled being battles
A stone-age status quo.

(IV)

Leonardo da Vinci,
Michelangelo,
Picasso,

Sculpt anew for me a horizon of roses
Agreeable
To the tenets on the tablet of Moses.

Distill into our day
In manageable
       doses

The drips of hope that bake breath
       into our human noses.

In the palatial palanquin of dawn,
       Nadine,
       a new born babe, dozes!

CHRIS HANI -

ATOP
THE TABLE MOUNTAIN OF DESTINY,
I HEAR THE CHIMES OF SANITY

LIKE
THE MSHENGUVILLE MARIGOLDS

OF AMEDEO MODIGLIANI
IN THE UNHURRIED GUILLOTINE
OF TIME.

(V)

Nadine Gordimer,

Your career, like a crusading Cassirer,
Is a carrier of our bow and arrow
      and our cause.

As a seer
Piercing the shaft of a shimmering
      barrier,

Your chants toe no line,
    you hold your own.
Like a bold Rhinehold bulldozer,
You charge on all fours, you know
    no pause.
Your heartbeat trots on,
Like a twenty-second century

    Trotsky,
Against even prehistoric forces.

STEVE BIKO,

ATOP
THE TABLE MOUNTAIN OF DESTINY
I HEAR THE CHIMES OF SANITY
LIKE
THE MORAKABE BOUGAINVILLEAS
OF FRANSISCO GOYA
IN THE UNHURRIED GUILLOTINE
OF TIME.

(VI)

You challenge the barbaric forces
      to toss their coins;
Moreover, with your left hand,
      you plant
A molotov cocktail of woven words
And incantation against the loins
      of their lores

      and laws.
Like a mesmerized Eldorado Park
      matador
Breaking down dehumanising boulders
      and doors, your
Images demystify the act of breathing.
Your sentences
      release the human soul
From their sentence of house arrest.

NADINE GORDIMER,

Like
An anti-Goliath pebble from Golgotha,
Thunder and lightning join hands
      with your words
      to protest

Against what the Gods and Gordimers
      of our preceding centuries,
      detest:

Ethnic cleansing and constitutional
      incest.

SOL PLAATJIE:

ATOP
THE TABLE MOUNTAIN OF
        DESTINY

I HEAR THE CHIMES OF SANITY

LIKE THE JABULANI
        FRESCOES
OF HENRI TOULOUSE-LAUTREC

IN THE UNHURRIED GUILLOTINE

OF TIME.

(VII)

Like a Gutenburg warrior-princess
    who sculpts the word
To multiply and spread a thought,
Like a sower that goes forth to sow
    seeds in starving
    souls,
Like a democratised angel
    released
    on secondment among men,

Like the century-mandated William
    Gates,
Nadine Gordimer,
    wielding the crowbar of
An iron will,
    throws ajar
All the bloody Brandenburg gates
    of the human soul,

Unchaining handcuffed thoughts and

Censored dreams

To rush onto the rebellious boulevard
Of fates.

Behind the prison bars of horrific human
Hates,

Man's decent destiny no longer hungers
And faints!

FRANTZ FANON
FRANTZ FANON

ATOP

THE TABLE MOUNTAIN OF DESTINY,

I SEE THE
SIGNATURES IN THE HELICOPTER
SKIES,

I READ
THE WRITING ON THE SHARPEVILLE
WALL,

I FEEL
THE SOWETAN PULSE OF UBUNTU,

I HUM
THE TINABANTU CHANT OF LIBERTY,

I HEAR
THE SQUATTERERCAMP CHIMES
OF SANITY

IN THE UNHURRIED GUILLOTINE
OF TIME

IN THE UNHURRIED GUILLOTINE
OF TIME.

(Pretoria-Johannesburg 12th - 15th November, 1998)

from:

RHODODENDRONS IN DONKEYDOM
-Fanfare for Cabral
-Watu Wazuri

Preface to
RHODODENDRONS IN DONKEYDOM

"Rhododendrons in Donkeydom," a long poem
in over twenty rivers, deals with the plight of creators,
the flowers of humanity, in human society
and human history: more often than not, their fate
is not dissimilar to that of rhododendrons in donkeydom
- the kingdom of donkeys. The creators
are musicians, artists, social revolutionaries, scientists
and architects.

FANFARE FOR CABRAL

I

Chaka the Zulu
Kwame Nkrumah
Eduardo Mandlane
Murtala Mohammed

Sojourner Truth

RHODODENDRONS FOR YOU -

Malcolm X
Martin Luther King
Che Guevara
Mahatma Ghandi

Sojourner Truth
RHODODENDRONS FOR YOU -
ODUDUWA

See me Lakayana with my spear -
The spear which my grandfather gave me,
My grandfather who fought the Whiteman,
The Whiteman who stole our lands,
The Whiteman who thinks he's here for ever.

See me Lakayana with my spear -
The beautiful ones are now being born.
The table mountain and the jacaranda tree

Are quarrelling over the correct spelling
Of our second name.

SEE ME LIKE A HYENA IN YOUR FEARS.

II

Amilcar Cabral
May his tribe increase -
(Like the bees and breeze in our trees)-
Awoke one night from a deep dream
Of peace

(Was felled one morning into a swift dance
of war)

seer-sorcerer...
soothsayer-prophet...
He must not live
and pollute the people's minds.

III

I see the blood -
and I can entertain no silence
I see the blood -
and I cannot support any silence.

The two white South African policemen
Half-balance you off your feet,
With your armpits on their shoulders.

Raw pain is a fascist tyrant galloping
Roughshod through all the fire-raped
Hamlets of your handsome Azanian face.
The blood gushing from your thigh
And breaking through the cloth
Is thick and fresh on your blue trouser,
Splashing unto your bare feet
That have never been on speaking terms
With sandal or shoe.

Your carriers - one is without his cap -
Grip-carry their guns with their 2 free hands.

Where are they taking you?
WHERE ARE THEY TAKING YOU?

IV

And again the pistol too has lied -
All the villages and hamlets have cried.

Over their beloved Amilcar Cabral
PISTALET I SNOVA SOLGAL.

O dangling dew of dawn
O slow-singing cloud-kite of sky,
O low-loitering calabash of wind,

How long's our song been bombed?
How long's the light been knifed?
How long's the dove been down?

V

Sailing through the air

(and charging between the parted thighs
of the rainbow-thunder urinating
Onto next decade's dawn-horizon,

The shrill cries of the warriors
Gather echo-momentum

With the force of bricks
With the decidedness of sticks,

And unto the ear-drums
Of the enemy,
Crash.

They shall know no peace.
They shall fight like eunuchs
In a harem.

VI

Amilcar Cabral -
I too have seen him across the farmfields
At dawn
Striding - the peasant warrior -

Destabilizing bridges,
Tendering flowers,
Whispering certain addresses
Into the ears
Of the gathering tongues of fire
And leading cattle to pastures and springs
And singing songs that summon sounds
That pour pails of pure well-water
Unto the tired spirit.

VII

Tomorrow in court you are all to plead
The taflatse amendment, according to which
All land is to be handed back to the people.

Tell the others, don't quote me. Goodbye.

Every home is to keep its oil lamp burning.

We have advised the sun not to appear
Until all land is handed back to the people.

Go spread the word. Don't quote me. Goodbye.

Knives will tonight change the addresses
Of the eldest children of the enemy -
All the land must be given back to the people.

TELL THE PEOPLE. DON'T QUOTE ME. GOODBYE.

VIII

O Vasco da Gamma,

Though the cries of Cabral crawl
From your incinerators of sin,
The cudjel-crushed chants of the people,
Soaring like foul-fanged serpentine spears,

In mid-air, wiggle,

Becoming gravity-hammering gamma rays,
Piercing and puncturing the shrinking
Stammering
Soldier spine
Of sick-souled parasitical portugalian Antonio
De Spinola

In Guinea Bissau
In Mozambique
In Angola.

IX

God gave Noah the rainbow sign -
No more water, the fire next time.

O SAKUMO O ODUDUWA

The assegais
        Of Lubenga's elephant hunter,
The assegais
        Of Nyanda the spirit medium,
The assegais
        Of Nagubi the lion's claw,
The assegais
        Of the Pupu River
The assegais of Soweto whisper:

NAMIBIA ZIMBABWE AZANIA

There is a shit-storm coming
There is a shit-storm coming

THERE IS A SHIT-STORM COMING

X

AMILCAR CABRAL,

I see your tribe increase,
Underneath the guerrilla boot of time,
Whiteman,
Your dream,
Dollar-infested, is but as safe as an egg...

AIN'T WORTH A DIME.

WATU WAZURI

to B.B. Attuquayefio

I

When all the blue is gone out
of the sky,
and the remaining hue is nothing
to fly a kite by,

birdsong
is the green lawn
of spring

on which the ears laze.

Upon the nile of my soul,
the lullaby of the flutist
floats

like a kite at dawn.

Ray Charles
and Stevie Wonder

you are acquainted with the
laughter of the thunder
but not with the look and
the smile of her lightening
that will meander

like the singing leap-year spine
of the sexy celestial belly dancer.

Like a Bobodiulasso kite
Commissioned by the Supreme Council

of the clouds
and the moonlight

and the ten toes and ten fingers
of the horizon of the soul,

you only wander and wonder -

you do not see
the world
you sing about.

Waumbaji,
Waumbaji
Watu Wazuri -
Rhododendrons in donkeydom.

II

Beethoven . . .
Beethoven . . .

you do not hear the songs
you sing about the world
you see.

Waumbaji,
Waumbaji,
Watu Wazuri -

Rhododendrons in donkeydom.

III

Miriam Makeba . . .
Miriam Makeba . . .

She shall not savour
the air and the soil of the land
that fuels and fires
her soul into song.

Miriam Makeba,

her spirit shall never waver.
Lonely in the cave-canyon-kraal
of labour,

her soul seasonally floats home,

stealthily sucks
of her motherland's
midnight breasts,
bursts forth into new births of song,
steeling the spirit
of her people
panting and prancing

in the dormant
volcano-dungeon
of racialist dung
and human wrong.

Waumbaji,
Waumbaji,
Watu Wazuri -
Rhododendrons in donkeydom.

IV

Osagyefo Kwame Nkrumah,

O spirit on an errand,
O spirit on an errand,

no sooner had you folded your mat
and gone beyond the corn-fields

than the Victoria falls
the namib desert
and the table mountain

burst out
in tears
and fire,

and the towncrier and his gong
and the eagle soaring in flight
burst out into fight and into song,
guinea bissau, angola -

mozambique, angola -
guinea Bissau, angola -
mozambique, angola

A LUTA CONTINUA
A LUTA CONTINUA

Waumbaji,
Waumbaji,
Watu Wazuri -
Rhododendrons in donkeydom.

from
TINKONGKONG! AYAWASO!

dedicated to…

… osagyefo kwame nkrumah and chaka the zulu
… tetteh quarshie and attoh quarshie
… aafokai tawiah and mariam makeba
… guy warren and afewerk tekle
… jawa apronti and mofolo bulane
… asare brown and amanor dseagu
… william conton and kofi asare opoku
… willie abraham and ayikwei armah
… the workers, peasants and youth of Africa
… the revolutionary people of Algeria

EVENSONG AT SOWETO

tinkong kong kong !
tinkong kong !

tinkong kong kong !
tinkong kong !

tinkong kong kong !
tinkong kong !

nye hea awo
nye hea awo
okaikoi ke ewebii mli ba ee
nye hea awo
nye hea awo
okaikoi ke ewebii mli ba ee
okaikoi ke ewebii mli ba ee

nkosi sikelela afrika

nye hea awo
nye hea awo
okaikoi ke ewebii mli ba ee
nye hea awo
nye hea awo
okaikoi ke ewebii mli ba ee
okaikoi ke ewebii mli ba ee
nkosi sikelela i afrika
nkosi sikelela i afrika

nko - si - sikelela
nko - si - sikelela

volcano in labour. earthquake on midnight beat
burn. cleanse. burn. erase. burn. burn.
uproot every blessed earthly taproot
amphibian Lucifer. iscariot judas
carnivorous cannibal. avoirdupois
and your Pontius Pilate my foot

ave maria. ave maria
Africa Africa... O Africa

I am. I am a sane martyr. I am mau mau
I am a violent avatar. I am shouting: au au

Sometimes only silence can sing
The song only the deaf can hear

Anaaa te, anaaa nme -
Anaaa nme, anaaa te -
Wobaa na te, wobaa na nme
Wobaa na te, wobaa na nme
Wobaa na te ke nme
the left washes the right
and the right washes the left.

my toe, my foe
my toe, my foe
it is the toe that trips.

when your conscience takes
a penalty kick against the
goal of your deeds and dreams

you may leave behind
the same old lord

and the same old god
the same old gong
and the same old song

only send me

another dream
a different dream

upon the grasslands green
of brave new Ghana,

shall we garner the manna
growing in the garden.

o land that is virgin
o sea that is serene

I am rearing to see the dove
that comes to kiss the land at dawn
I am rearing to see the song
that calls our name in the dream of dawn

oburumankoma
oburumankoma
oburumankoma ee

oburumankoma ee
odapagyan ee
osun ee
osun nekyir nnyiaboa

wild like fire... fall as the tree
wild like fire... free as the air
wild like fire...

      fire that
            races across the sea
            and razes down the wall
      fire that
            suffocates savanna
            and fossilizes forest

      fire that
            fractures rock
            and paralyses the path

nkrangpong nkrangpong
ashiedu keteke
ashiedu keteke

afrikapong afrikapong
ashiedu keteke
ashiedu keteke

odom ni amanfo

anaaa nme, anaaa te -
anaaa te, anaaa nme -
monka ntoa

monka ntoa

asante kotoko
angola kotoko
nigeria kotoko
sudan hu kotoko
botswana kotoko
morocco kotoko
afrika kotoko
guinea hu kotoko

kum apem a, apem beba
kill apem and apem will come
monka ntoa
monka ntoa
kwame nkrumah lo
sane ko mli do mi ee

sane ko mli do mi...
ei, algeria lo!

sane ko mli do mi ee
sane ko mli do mi...

ei, algeria lo!
sane ko mli do mi ee
sane ko mli do mi...

nkosi sikelela i afrika
nkosi sikelela i afrika

nko - si - sikelela
nko - si - sikelela
o, Namibia lo !
sane ko mli do mi ee
sane ko mli do mi...

afrika lo okropong ni
nkrumah lo okropong ni
efine ke, esani ele ebii ayikule
ele ebii ayikule, agro beye yie
o ele ebii ayikule, agro beye yie.

ELE EBII AYIKULE
AGRO BEYE YIE...

nye hea awo
nye hea awo
okaikoi ke ewebii mli ba ee
nye hea awo

nye hea awo okaikoi ke ewebii mli ba ee
okaikoi ke ewebii mli ba ee

nkosi sikelela i afrika
nkosi sikelela i afrika

nko - si - sikelela
nko - si - sikelela

MANDELA THE SPEAR

Dedicated To All African Freedom
Fighters And Winnie Mandela

I

Within my lifetime,
Golden
Like a kitchen saucepan-saluted
Egg,

Dawn

INDEED HAS BROKEN OUT
UPON A STARTLED WORLD .

From under the mortar-bomb
                blockade of silence
                        of the three decades,
Like Kwame Nkrumah
                through the uncomfortable
                        James Fort
Overwhelmed
                Gaping prison gates,
Like unyielding
                Infant plant
                        Spearing -
Bursting out
        Of crackling concrete,

He, at last,
        awakes
        and walks

Out,
Straight,
Like a delegated peasant magistrate
Summoned
By the streets.

He will
Legislate
On the Sakumo-Larabanga silhouette

Of our soul's
                    cleanest slate

A common people's

                    humanest state.

The flag of the free is finally
Unfurled!
How many children have they not
Savaged!
How many of our souls have they
Not felled!

II

AND ON THE THIRD DAY,
HE

AROSE AGAIN FROM THE
DEAD,

And went out into the multitude
Among whom
His multi-decadal stony silence
Committed
An instant suicide

Before
A flabbergasted century.

He shattered
Asunder

(Like knee-kicking
Ogunian Niyi Osundare,
Who dares
Like the dare-devil
World-winning Winifred Mandela,

To annihilate

The totemic anti-atomic sun-system
Of the soul-destabilizing
Sound system)

The whirlwind whisperings
That would plunder
The ancient commando-grove

Resolve

In our bewildered
Refugee-pilgrim nomadic bones.

The elements,
Femi Osofisan
Sufficiently affirms,
Will commit no cardinal blunder -
(Fill in the blanks. Command the land):

NATURE STILL ABHORS A VACUUM.

The flag of the free is finally
Unfurled!

How many children have they not
Savaged!
How many of our souls have they
Not felled!

III

The Pharaonic bells at Egypt's
Abu Simbel
         transmit
Territorial
Signals about Nelson Mandela.

The spear girls at the Ngorongoro
Crater
And the arrow boys
         of the Zimbabwe Ruins

Yell out the clenched-fist
Garland-salute for Nelson Mandela.

In the stone temples of Ethiopia's
Lalibela,
         the ancestral fighter-spirits
Of Chaka the Zulu
         and Kwame Nkrumah,
Amilcar Cabral
         and Moshoeshoe,
Dingaan and Prince Lumumba,
Samora Machel
         and Thomas Sankara,

In unison chant
An anthem-hymn for Nelson Mandela.

From the Cape

Now

Of the steadfast, unsleeping
Sharpeville Ghost,
From the Cape
Now of true and Soweto's Hope,

We
Stride aright.
We no longer grope.

Gather in the winds
In which our vision will bathe.

Roll-call the folks

Who in pain have kept the faith.
On top
Of
The Festus Iyayi Table Mountain
(There is no fainting)
We are mounting
The flag of the free
And

The spear of the Nation.

Gather in the winds
Of the legendary years.
Roll-call the folks
Assessed in blood and in tears.
On top
Of
The lone Steve Biko Table Mountain,
(There is no waiting)
We are mounting
The flag of the free
And

The Spear of the Nation.

A SOMERSAULT OF THE MIDNIGHT: NELSON MANDELA, THE AFRICAN WARRIOR

Behold the man, an anthill squatting
In the midst of the sea !
Behold the lord of the land whose basket

will hold all water !

Our enemies, squatting from afar, shouted:

abelenkpe !

You took and held your stand atop the

Table Mountain,

Releasing your Nile-splitting response

nketie nta !

Abelenkpe, nketie nta !
Abelenkpe, nketie nta !

They dug diabolical dungeons in which
They dared to dream of burying your
Breathing alive.

They schemed and dared to barricade

The borderless territories of your soul
Within boulders rivalling the heights
And width of the Zimbabwe Ruins.

In broad daylight they strove to wrap up
Your soul
In the heart-exploding confines of a fascist

Tarpaulin . . .
And within the belly of a whale, you staged
A somersault of the midnight.

You are the man who would smoke a pipe,
While seated on the tip of the barrel
Of a gun !

(Let them fire a thousand shots, and not
Even a single hair of any of our own would be
Touched !)

When you dig the soil, water
Always gushes up in wiling response !

(Let them fire a thousand shots, and not
Even a single hair of any of our own would
Be touched !)

Your struggles yield today fruits
And flowers as colourful
                    as the butterflies of Oyibi.

O African Warrior-lion, Madiba,

You it was who chased away with a thorny
                    crackling thundering whip

The filthy money-changers from within

                    the temple of our land.

From the corners of the planet earth,
Your saga is told and retold as a tale.

The very elements chant the anthem
                    of your praises.

O African Warrior-lion, Madiba !

Wielding the Herero-Zimbabwe singing

Spear

Of Osagyefo the Kwame Nkrumah,

You

Sacked and scattered enslavers
Of our people

From the face of our sacred land.

Our people offer you their crown !
Our people heap a hyssop upon your
Shoulders !

Step forth and accept their offering !
Step forward and don the garland !

Madiba, behold the crown !
Madiba, behold the hyssop !

III

ON THE SOULSCAPE OF THE BULLET TRAIN

to Daisaku Ikeda,
Satoru Tsuchiya and Kazuko Asai

1. Far squatting, fabled

    Mount fuji,
    it is from your realm
    that the flowers flee

    on a schizophrenic
    century's shinkansen,

    to deposit their serenity
    at a Shinto shrine in Shinjuku
    where the seven hundred red lanterns
    loom like hanging crabs on parade.

    Fair mount fuji,
    it is from your bosom
    the moon blossoms.

2. On the soulscape
    of the bullet train,

    cherry blossoms chant
    the twenty-first century's
    refrain:

    I AM JAPAN.
    I AM JAPAN.

    I am a country with a plan.
    I am a country on the run.
    I brook no bounds.
    I detest any ban on the thinking of man.

    I AM JAPAN. I AM JAPAN.

Gazing into my jade of Buddha-san,
I am racing mankind's rising sun.

Like an encyclopaedia salesman from Isfahan,
I am journeying, I'm jogging, I'm on the run.
Like the Akosombo turbines of the Kianji dam,
I'm sweating, I could do with a portable fan.

I AM JAPAN. I AM JAPAN.

I am a country on the run.
Like the restless roving sun,
My imagination's on a safari

ACROSS THE THOUGHT-IRRIGATED
FIELDS OF THE THINKERS' KALAHARI,

Across the kitchen chimneys
                        of calabash-carving
                                Kojimachi,
Along the populated pavements
                        of sandstone-tatooing
                                Shinjuku,
Across the archaic arcades
                        of canoe-calling
                                Okayama,
Through the quiet thoroughfares
                        of bamboo-bangled
                                Omotesando,
Over the Sunday sands
Of tea-sipping
Akasaka-mitsuke

Through the garden gates
                        of charcoal-chisselling
                                Ichigaya,
Alongside the million millipedes
                        of moat-admiring
                                Marounouchi,

Into the green ancient groves
                    of yam-peeling
                              Yasukuni,
Over the bold babbling brooks
                    of Buddha-brooding
                              Budokan,

I AM JAPAN. I AM JAPAN.

I am a country where a man
Works for solitude in the sun.

I
AM
JAPAN.

A TEA CEREMONY FOR THE NEUTRON BOMB

dedicated to
Prof. Alexander A. Kwapong
and Mr. Kobo Abe

Yuri Tanimoto,
in Kyoto's Heian-jingu century old garden
of perfect peace and tranquillity,
your blood-red spider web-delicate umbrella,
Yuri Tanimoto,
rains red from your charcoal-black hair
to your white cloth covered toe,
Yuri Tanimoto.

You sit awaiting the guests
to the century's tea ceremony
in your glowing white kimono,
Yuri Tanimoto, in the soul-soothing lap
of patient water, giggling green
pine needles, humble footpaths
and contented stone.

1

KAII HIGASHIYAMA

let us drink tea
let us hold the bowl with both hands.
bamboo grove in the moonlit night.
waning spring. pond in the garden.
rising moon. moonlit blossoms.
dawn.

KAII HIGASHIYAMA,

forest with a white horse.
echo of trees. evening of stillness.
watery green. frozen pond. snow castle.

lake. evening bell. misty town.
window.

2

KAII HIGASHIYAMA

distant view of mountain lake. autumn
leaves in the valley. cliff. sound of the
tide. two moons. glow of white night.
early summer, tree spirits.
blue symphony.

3

KAII HIGASHIYAMA

How much water do we need to pour
into the teapot of love and sanity
to brew the healing tea
for the soul of the age ?

Twentieth century, what is the matter ?
Twentieth century, stop your stammer !

It takes about ten million
droplets
to make a raindrop.

Go and ask Einstein.
Go and ask Yukawa.

4

They have, you say,
uncle Alexander Kwapong,
in man-planned,
pathfinding jewel Japan,
lots of water.
They have, too, I agree,

Professor Kwapong,
multi-ton silos of light
in the mind.

Humiko Yashima
hears the twenty-first century sound
its guernica-gong:
humanity must answer -
destiny
shall be no more of a ping-pong.

5

O sweet seventeen year old Humiko Yashima,
Your english-speaking high school heart
sets mine ashimmer
as your umbrella-bearing sisters' eyes
register a glimmer.
May the seven great temples of Nara
bring us all nearer
for our souls to hold hands
in a humane hiroshima.

May the fifteen hundred stone laterns
of the white deer shrine shine.

6

Our fate dangles over fangs of fire.

Disentangle, Kenzo Tange,
our dreams from fear,
our faith from the gutter,
our hair from the thorns.

Kenzo Tange,
we knock on your window,
we cross the Tsukuru bridge
to come to you.

Kenzo Tange,
the birds have fallen quiet,
only the wind continues to blow,
the fires of hope have ceased to glow.

We cross the Tsukuru bridge
to come to you.

7

Doctor Yukawa,
bring out your candle -
we are trapped in the century's
suffocating elevator.

Yukawa, you do not cower.
Your every breath has been, Yukawa,

a fearless fortune-teller's jump
from a Kiyomizu verandah.
From the tall Himeji White Heron
castle tower, Yukawa,
we hear your guernica-gong
of the eleventh hour:
those with cotton wool between
their thighs
should never jump over fire.

8

When human fright urinates
the uranium

of indifference
over the disciplined basket-weaving
fingers of the pregnant girl,

When human fright urinates
the uranium
of indifference

over the breasts of the humming
young woman bathing in the waters
of the flattered early morning river,

when human fright urinates
the uranium
of indifference
over the ears of the neighing horse
grazing alone in the rolling fields,

the peace of the rose petal in love
is shattered between the anvil
and the hammer -

plateau of pain, rest in peace . . .

the peace of the cherry blossom in bloom
is shattered between the anvil
and the hammer -

plateau of pity, rest in peace . . .

the soul of the green in the grasshopper's
neck is imprisoned in the steel-melting oven -

wilderness of cinders, rest in peace . . .

smiling is knifed in the heart,
sunlight and love are gored in the open -

O, MAMA !
AARHG, NAGASAKI !
O, MAMA MIA !
SHHH, HIROSHIMA!

9

When human conscience urinates
the uranium
of indifference
over the sweating skin of the rice
harvesting father-in-law,

when human conscience urinates
the uranium
of indifference
over the hamlet-building shoulders
of the whistling grandmother,

when human conscience urinates
the uranium
of indifference
over the face of the lake forever

endeavouring to seduce
the unsteady clouds into marriage,
the peace in the ancestry of a song
is shattered between the anvil
and the hammer -

plateau of plain, rest in peace . . .

the soul of the green in the grasshopper's
neck is imprisoned in the steel-melting oven -

wilderness of cinders, rest in peace . . .

smiling is knifed in the heart,
sunlight and love are gored in the open -

O, MAMA!
AARHG, NAGASAKI !
O, MAMA MIA !
SHHH, HIROSHIMA!

10

when human reason urinates
the uranium
of indifference
over the heaven-seeking forehead
of the maize-pounding pestle,

when human reason urinates
the uranium
of indifference
over the window-cleaner's ears,

when human reason urinates
the uranium
of indifference
over the innocent lips of the schoolboy
playing his grandfather's village harmonica,

the peace of the butterfly in flight
is shattered between this anvil
and the hammer -

plateau of pain, rest in peace . . .

the peace of the canary in song
is shattered between the anvil
and the hammer -

plateau of pity, rest in peace . . .

the soul of the mauve in twilight's cheek
is imprisoned in the marble-melting oven -

wilderness of cinders, rest in peace . . .

breathing is knifed in the heart
sunlight and love are gored in the open -

O, MAMA!
AARHG, NAGASAKI!
O, MAMA MIA!
SHHH, HIROSHIMA!

(11/9/81 - 15/9/81 Hiroshima -Tokyo)

BIRDS: REGINA AND BETTY

Leaving behind
The rainsoaked, leaf-kissed
Streets,
Invisible windmills,
Technicolored farm fields
And territorial boundaries
Of warm-bodied, embrace-poised
Amsterdam,

We soar onto the level
Beyond the clouds (whiter than
The bathroom walls and generous
Folded towels of the Golden Tulip
Barbizon Hotel, awash
In Brenghel pastel colours),

Swiftly and courageously
Imitating
The fish floating inside water,
The bird floating on the air
Like a seasoned masquerader
Waltzing on aerial stilts.

After a sudden airborne
Encounter,
(Unprogrammed, unchoreographed)
With the inquisitive beak of a bird,
Gate-crashing
Like a blind soothsayer

Into our charted flight path
(Window-scaling to peep into

Our shower or bathroom?)

Wing-kissing to feel our lips,

We are blown back to base
("As you were!")
By the consoling wind of sanity
Sheathed and concealed
In the computer console
To go back and buckle our shoe
Again,

Zip our trouser's fly again,
And adjust the handkerchief
In our breast pocket.

We return
Into the outstretched
Arms
Of an Amsterdam
That understands.

No harm.
No cause for alarm.
Enjoy the charms
Of Amsterdam.

DAR ES SALAAM:
HAIZEL AT THE 38TH PARALLEL

AaSalaam Aleikum, Dar Es Salaam!
AaSalaam Aleikum, Dar Es Salaam!

Ataa Kwamina

It is one o'clock now in Kaesong in Korea

a well-tended summer garden
of a five course lunch is spread out
on the moonlight-valley embroidery
on the innocently white table-cloth,
provoking the long-starved saliva
that like monsoon-time waterfalls
must be rampaging

in the gentlemanly jaws of friends
who are here seated.

Like a shy bamboozled flower-buying
stranger
in a bamboo-necklaced Bangkok
I bang my beautiful fork's bony thighs
against the resounding ribcage
of an incorrigible teetotaler's
empty yawning glass,

and rising from my floor-scratching chair,
claim
and colonize the floor for a toast.

Korean cutlery stop playing
their far eastern cricket
with Korean cuisine.

Our convoy of blue brown and green
mercedes benz cars

like an uncommissioned antarctica expedition
crawls out of drowsy Pyongyang at dawn,

and like wise millipedes, progress
on the frost-bitten ice-encrusted roads
like the manure-cart dragging
water buffaloes that we overtake
on our single-minded march
TOWARDS THE 38TH PARALLEL
in Kaesong
in Korea.

Ataa Kwamina
(national captain and champion
of the hockey pitch and calculating stick,
cricket oval and thundering bat,
long jump pit and sturdy legs,
and football field and elusive feet,)

Starting with Accra, then Coutonou
then Tripoli, then Moscow and then Irkurst,
we had jumped over

national borders
(built on the stamped pages of passports
and the uninviolatable visa,
flapping flags and aneamic anthems,
custom officers and scanning machines,
screening doors and transit hotels -
out of which you are not allowed to telephone),

had overcome
natural boundaries -
rivers and lakes, mountains and jungles,
dizzy heights of clouds
and datelines and jetlags

and now head towards
an artificial border

that, like a sharpened butcher's knife

in the hand of a magician,

(against a backdrop of loudspeakers
in the cold armpits of mute mountains
and soldiers and soldiers),

has sliced up
into two almost equal halves
the Korean soul.

I realise suddenly:
the twenty-fourth of January
marks your own
but natural border -
(Thank God - no sentries. And no guns.
No passports. No flags. No Anthems.)

Today at dawn
(faraway from home
faraway from Doreen and Emmanuel,
faraway
from Mercy, faraway from Abigail
and Joseph and their loving mama)

You reached the 56th parallel
of your soul's horizontal marathon,
towards its bountiful-land gracious source.

YOUR PASSPORT IS YOUR HEART.

Place of birth: Odoben, in the Central Region,
Ghana.
Place of issue: mother's 9 month old womb.
Date of issue: 24th January, 1928.
Issuing Authority: The government of the
Universe.
Issuing Agent: Mama and Papa.

YOUR VISA IS IN YOUR NOSTRILS.

YOU CROSS THIS PARALLEL TONIGHT.
YOU CROSS THIS PARALLEL TONIGHT.

Happy Birthday, Ataa Kwamina!
Careful crossing, Ataa Kwamina!

And lots of love.

KWABENYA

To live at Kwabenya
And be without a European donkey
Is really to return to grassroots,
To be one with the grasshopper,
To be one with the rabbit,
To be one with the praying mantis,

The frog, the hare and the grasscutter -

And in that context,
Mobility is equal to

Your destination (as the crow flies)
Divided by the possibility of the availability of a
Lift,
Multiplied by the current position of the sun,

Multiplied by the philosophy of the tortoise,
Divided by the territorial geometrics of the snail,

Plus the 'to be or not to be'
Protocol politics of the chameleon.

Preface to "Agegeyan Gethsemane"

This poem, written from Accra - Ghana - West Germany - London - and then back to Accra over the period from 29th September, 1980 to 30th October, 1980, proved to be prophetic.

Agege, a suburb in Nigeria, is a slum area in Lagos. Being a lowcost area, most Ghanaians who went to Nigeria, found themselves living there. The name Agege thus become a symbol of Ghanaian migration to Nigeria as a result of their sudden wealth following the discovery of large quantities of oil. At the same time (1978 - 1983) the Ghanaian economy had gone down, and it was characterised by basic shortage and lack of essential commodities on the market, such as milk, sugar, toilet roll, etc.

Aliens Compliance Order
This was an Executive Order given in 1971 that all those who did not have the necessary residential documents should leave. Thousands of non-Ghanaians, particularly those from West Africa were expelled one night from Ghana. Some of them had been born here. In these circumstances the people involved had to sell their properties cheap.

1983: In 1983, President Shehu Shagari of Nigeria announced that all aliens without valid residential documents in Nigeria should leave. Consequently about one million Ghanaians had to be repatriated.

Naa Dzeringa was a Mamprusi chief in Northern Ghana who in ancient days was so security-conscious to the extent that he built a thick five-foot wall around his traditional capital, Nalerigu. He was so anxious to get this was completed that he used substances like hone, shea butter and even the bodies of those who worked out themselves and collapsed.

AND NOW TO END THE WORLD NEWS:
AGEGEYAN GETHSEMANE

from the long poem, "The Gong Gongs
of Mount Gongtimano")

dedicated to
Hamida Harrison,
Late J. Bekunuru Kubayanda,
Late J.A. Dwamena

I

The gong-gong groans; agoo ...
The song says: salaam ...

THE LAND LIES ALONE.

The moat moans: shaman!
The soul says: I am!
The gong-gong groans: agoo...

A mummified mirage still murmurs at me,
and refuses and refuses to remain mum!
It points out visions the souls seek to see,
it whispers the melody the spirit seeks to hum:

the horizon is horizontal
the landmarks are monumental
the landscape is simply lying -
my horizon is rising !
my horizon is rising !

II

The dreams of last night
must be stepping out of the taxi
right now

in front of the door
of the insurance company
that has promised to guarantee
that they do not wither
or shrivel in the heat of time
or in the cold of neglect.

But I have every reason to suspect
that they may not have enough funds
to pay the taxi driver ...

THE RIDE HAS TAKEN SO LONG!

III

We've checked our dream through
customs -
In this village and age, what
are the customs?

IV

The frightened sun at noon, fleeing home
like a calabash-helmetted neurotic kangaroo,
slams the half-unhinged doomsay door

in the now-anaemic face of our dream
in the eleventh season of its hunger strike,
flinging over its supersonic shoulder
a boomragoid consolation:

> we shall get back to you
> after some consultation
> and instructions
> from our sponsors.

V

NONSENSE
AND NONSENSE
AND NONSENSE AGAIN

I SEE the solemnly sagging Ghanaian sun
struggling along the dehydrated horizon
like a dunkwa-on-offin trotro lorry driver
hunting for five and a half teaspoonfuls
of brakefluid
at the Sunday afternoon Kokompe
Pandora box miscellaneous market.

I SEE
the alarm-clock alerted spareparts dealer
in his dazzling midnight Mercedes Benz
drive out onto the first class roads
with a pigax in his air-conditioned car
to sprinkle and sink
pigax-sculptured
potholes

into the coughing chest
and fractured ribs
of the Arizona Canyon
roads.

I SEE all the markets become
on akwatia goldmine for the seller
and an overcrowded slaughter house

of the soul
for the frightened and nervous
consumer.

I SEE
the peasant farmer lose his family farm
to the octopus-tentacled
seedy cedi-soiled city creditor.

I HEAR
of tons of tomatoes stranded and rotting away
in farms far away from cities constipated
with able-bodied young people hawking
dog-chains, chewing gun
and contact breakal points
in the sunbaked streets,

where dead traffic lights
and mortally-priced tomatoes
squat unmoving and unmoved,
like monuments
of a sorry mini-century.

I SEE
one hen-manufactured egg
literally grow within a week
to be worth its weight
in pure Ghanaian gold.

I SEE
my Lord and Chief Justice Apaloo,

almost
impaled on his Presidential promise,
plunge,
lungs-long and aqualung-less,
into his water-logged
legislative waterloo.

I OVERHEAR
in the oven-hot streets
youngmen muttering to themselves,

like some akwasidae-rejected sorcerers
angered by the slowly-swelling stomach
of a sacrifice-starved
River Bosumtwi,

about the scorching cost of charcoal
and the uncontrollably demented price
of the greedily dented new America
tin of gari.

I SEE
an innocent looking sunshine-accosted
tin of the most meek milk
become too hot
for the financially anaemic consumer
fingers
of the man who has severed
all diplomatic and consular relations
with his heartless bank manager's
domain.

I RECOGNIZE
the voice of my next door neighbour
moaning in the worried wind, wading
like a drunken Nakpanduri Fulani gipsie
through the hanging golden leaves
and the tall-standing green grasses

(like the spirit of God
moving on the face of the waters)

SHOUT WITH THE SHARPNESS OF
CUTLASSES:

Just what, please,
is the correct revised address
of God?

and who the devil there in hell
is hiding
the official forwarding address
of Jesus Christ?

I COME
upon whole families carpentering
into their sleeping rooms
and disponsable abode
of everynight in Bukom Square
and the Nima Highway

the lampless boundless free akies
and the wornout free streets
contoured by the invisible walls
which are the hospitable all-accepting
gutters of night
strangling the nostrils of the soul
with the tear-gas of stone-age stink.

I HEAR PIERCING
the dead silence of the communal midnight
the soul-suffocating insistent crying
of the child asking for bread and for milk,

AND I FEEL

the hiroshima bombs of helplessness,
frustration, sorrow and guilt
and the nagasaki bombs

of self-pity

and self-hate
devastate
into smithereens
and scatter asunder, like wedding
party confetti,

the lonely bridge of sanity dangling high
over the soul's unquiet River Kwai

in the volcano-veined
Krakatoa-tile
palpitating parental heart

of
mother
and
father.

VI

Aflao destablizes our toil
and manufacturers our poverty...
our future faints at Aflao
like a fugitive from freedom and sanity.

VII

The gods of Agege cannot ignore
the lonely beggar's Ghanaian tears
gravitating like stone-age graffiti
onto the horizon-canvas of conscience.

The gods of Agege cannot ignore
that it was God who created the human jaw
in both the man with the Swiss bank account
and the beggar chanting by the rich door.

In the hunter-haunted
oven-iglows of godless Agege,
gasps and groans silently congregate
in the guttered groins
of the Ghanaian soul
stepping stealthily across the naked night
and across the sleeping soil
of blood-soiled Agege ...

AGEGE MY GETHSEMANE!
AGEGE MY GUERNICA!
AGEGE MY GOLGOTHA!

Let not the savage enemy
garage and grills us
in this Gethsemane.

VIII

The agegeyan skulls in the gutters
of Golgotha
gather and holler at human nature
and the state of the soul's weather.

Sunny Okusson's fiery flugelhorn
of faith and fate farts
into our ear's gaping gate:

who owns the land and who holds the gold?
who tills the land and who eats the yam?

     and the cassava leaves hang
     green and green at Okponglo
     and the cassava trees stand ...
               grey and grey at Okponglo

who owns the land and who sells the cocoa?
who tills the land and who eats the corn?

who owns the land and who sells the timber?
who mans the land, who mans the borders?

and the cassava leaves hang
green and green at Okponglo
and the cassava trees stand ...
grey and grey at Okponglo

IX

And now to end the world news,
here are the mainpoints again:

1971 - Ghana has expelled all
        aliens; it is reported that
        most of them were from
        neighbouring Nigeria.

1972 -   It has been announced
          that the Ministry
          of Air of Ghana has directed
          that with immediate effect
          people whose income is
          below 400 Cedis a month
          should use cotton wool
          to block one of the nostrils
          to help the conservation of air
          which is in short supply.

1979 -   The Government of Ghana has
          described as false rumours
          circulating that yellow corn
          meant for animal feed is
          being used for human consumption.

1980 -   Ghanaians are abandoning
          Ghana in huge numbers.

1980 - The Passport office in Accra
          has been burnt down by
          an unidentified Ghanaian
          protesting the limitation of
          his freedom of movement
          guaranteed under the
          Constitution.

1980 -   Five Ghanaian nationals
          were among twenty persons
          reported dead of suffocation
          in Lagos while being conveyed
          to a magistrate court from a prison in
          a Black Maria carrying
          sixty suspects.

1980 - A bus load of teachers
        and their Nigerian
        recruiters were set
        on fire by their local
        village vigilante group
        near the Aflao border.

1980 - Ghana, which is already
        rich in reserves of gold,
        diamond and bauxite, has
        discovered gas in
        Saudi Arabian quantities.

1982 - Ghana has discovered
        oil hiding under the
        midnight mattresses
        of villagers in several
        parts of the country.

1983 - The Ghanaian authorities
        are erecting a Naa
        Dzeringa wall in their
        efforts to seal off their
        borders to check
        the onrush of both
        job-seeking foreigners
        and returning Ghanaians.

X

The morning marigolds gather again
in the mountain gardens of Gethsemane.
The midnight glories flower afresh
in the dawn-time fanfare for fairies.
And God in his goodness
is showering gold over Ghana again,

over the gorgeous contours of Ghana's lands
over all the mountain tops.

And the happy horizon again is aflame
with the timid light of rebirth,
the darkness again is departing
like a lover withdrawing at dawn
to the cricket's concerto
and the tadpole's tattoo.

The mist of morn is milky in the air,
the honey of hope is high in the head,
the bonfires of faith
are frolicking into force,

and a man shall not breathe
by bread alone,

and the soul shall not sing
for the seen alone,
but by every dream that drums
in the dungeons of distance,

but by every vision that totters
like a toddler in nappies,

venturing ahead into frontiers new
with pathfinders trodding in tow.

XI

I see him. I can see him now.
I have caught him at it.
He is doing it again.

> GOD AGAIN IS SPRINKLING
> THINGS
> ALL OVER THE PLACE

The gold of the soul, the jewels
        of the spirit,
the diamonds of the mind, the
        pearls of labouring hands,

the precious minerals of the
        earth
and the bounteous fruits
        of the fields ...
showers of blessings upon us.

The morning marigolds gather again
in the mountain gardens of Gethsemane.
The midnight glories flower a fresh
in the dawn time fanfare for fairies.

Amen

(Accra-Geneva-West Germany-London-Accra: 29/9/80 - 30/10/80)

POSTSCRIPT

Atukwei Okai continues to be invited to read his work to audiences in Africa, Europe, and around the world. The following is a selection of the performance history of some of the poems in this volume:

"THE ROSETTA STONE IN THE MEANTIME OF ETERNITY": The first world performance of the poem, **The Rosetta Stone In The Meantime of Eternity (dedicated with love to the African people, and to the founding fathers of the OAU),** was at the Special Poetry Evening organized and hosted by the Egyptian Minister of Culture, Mr. Farouk Hosni, at the Akhenaton Gallery, in Cairo, in honour of Okai the poet and visiting Chairman of the International Preparatory Committee (IPC) of the Pan African Writers' Association (PAWA) in February, 1988.

In February, 1988, I gave a performance of it at a dinner for about 50 writers, painters and others in the cultural world, in honour of the PAWA delegation, hosted by the Minister of Culture of Ethiopia, at a restaurant in Addis Ababa.

A rendition of the poem took place, in honour of the retiring Director-General of UNESCO, Mr. Amadou Mohtar M'Bow, at the Second Conference of the OAU Ministers of Culture in Ouagadougou, Burkina Faso, in March, 1988. Okai, Chairman of the International Preparatory Committee (IPC) of the Pan African Writers' Association (PAWA), invited to attend and brief the conference on the project for the creation of PAWA, was, as "the representative of the writers" the last of the five conference participants asked to speak in honour of Mr. M'Bow.

On 12th June, 2007, it fell to my lot to give a performance of **The Rosetta Stone In The Meantime of Eternity** at a State Burial Service conducted for Madam Fathia Nkrumah at the Forecourt of The State House in Accra.

On that occasion I announced the addition of the name of Madam Fathia Nkrumah thence forth to the list of dedicatees of the poem.

"THE BOND OATH OF UBUNTU": The first world performance of **Ubuntu** took place during the World Conference on Culture in Stockholm, Sweden at an Evening Cultural Programme in February, 1988; at it was performed also at **THE SECOND PAN AFRICAN**

WRITERS ASSOCIATION (PAWA) WORLD POETRY FESTIVAL, at the Great Hall, of the University of Ghana, Legon, on 1st November, 1999; the **GRADUATION CERE MONY** of the Herman Gmeiner International College, Tema, Ghana, on 28th May, 1988; at the **STATE BANQUET** given by President Nelson Mandela in honour of the Chilean President, at the State House, Pretoria, South Africa, on 10th November, 1998; at the **NADINE GORDIMER'S 75TH ANNIVERSARY SEMINAR,** Johannesburg, South Africa, on 12th November, 1998; at **THE GHANA HIGH COMMISSIONER'S RECEPTION** in honour of Ghana's Status as the Focus Country of the Zimbabwe International Bookfair 2000, at his Residence on 2nd August, 2000, in Harare, Zimbabwe; on **THE BBC WORLD SERVICE PROGRAMME "ART BEAT"** (Host: Kweku Sakyi Addo) 19th, 22nd, and 24th January, 2002); and the GBC/TV Interview programme, **KWEKU ONE-ONONE,** (hosted: by Kweku Sakyi Addo), Accra 22nd March, 2002.

I gave a reading of the poem at the CNN African Journalists of the Year Awards Sponsors' Dinner at the Arcadia Ballroom of the Westcliff Hotel, Johannesburg, South Africa (2004), which was under the distinguished patronage of Mr. Chris Cramer, the Managing Director of CNN International, Mr. Phil Molefe, the Head of the South African Broadcasting Corporation (SABC) and Mr. Edward Boateng, the Managing Director of Global Media Alliance and founder of the Awards. I performed it at the Opening Ceremony of a Conference for Political Parties in Africa, organized by the Institute of Economic Affairs, at the Golden Tulip Hotel, Accra, on 4th May, 2007.

"WATU WAZURI": I performed it at the **EASTERN HEMISPHERE OUTDOORING OF WATU WAZURI,** for the first Conference of ANC (South Africa) students, Lumumba Friendship University, Moscow, USSR, 6th August, 1977; and at the Ghana Association of Writers (GAW) Gala Evening of Poetry and Music for the **Western Hemisphere Outdooring of WATU WAZURI** at the Great Hall, University of Ghana, Legon, November 1977, (Chair: Prof. Joe Kubayanda).

"MANDELA THE SPEAR": It was performed by the Malaysian Minister of Transport and Communications at the special ceremony organized in honour of President Nelson Mandela during his visit to Malaysia; I performed the poem at **THE MANDELA FORUM,** immediately after Nelson Mandela's Address, during his first official visit to Ghana, the Accra International Conference Centre, on 7th

November, 1991. The performance of the poem was the only other item on the programme. The event was broadcast live on State Television.

I performed the poem at a mass meeting at the Kwame Nkrumah Circle, Accra, on 11th March, 1990, to mark the release of Nelson Mandela from prison.

"A SOMERSAULT OF THE MIDNIGHT: NELSON MANDELA THE AFRICAN WARRIOR": The 13th International Poetry Festival in Medellin, Colombia, South America, and the 1st Worldwide Summit of Poetry for the Peace of Colombia, took place in June, 2003. One of the poems Okai performed there was **A Somersault of the Midnight: Nelson Mandela the African Warrior**. The poem, originally composed in the Ga language and translated into English, was performed in both languages on the occasion of the conferment of an Honorary Doctorate degree on former President Nelson Mandela by the University of Ghana, at the Special Conferment Ceremony at the Great Hall, Legon, in 2002.

NOTES TO THE POEMS

"THE ROSETTA STONE IN THE MEANTIME OF ETERNITY"

This poem was composed in Cairo during the one week that the Egypt Minister of Culture, Mr. Farouk Hosni, needed to organize a reading for me at the Akhenaton Gallery in Cairo. It was first performed there on 22nd February, 1988 and published in Arabic translation in the Al-Ahram newspaper.

At the Egyptian Museum, during a tour of historical sites and monuments, I had learnt that the Rosetta Stone, an ancient Egyptian irregularly-shaped stone of black basalt, was found near the town of Rosetta (Rashid) by a Frenchman in August 1799, and is now in the British Museum. Inscribed in two languages, Egyptian and Greek, and three writing systems, hieroglyphics, demotic script and the Greek alphabet, it provided a key to the translation of Egyptian hieroglyphics writing.

Sando Anoff: The son of the Ghana High Commissioner in Cairo, Dr. Anoff.

Samouri and Babatou: They were notorious for their exploits during the history of the slave trade in the Gold Coast. They dominated the trade in Northern Gold Coast.

Sakkara: It is one section of the great necropolis of Memphis, the Old Kingdom capital. The kings of the 1st Dynasty, as well as that of the 2nd Dynasty, are mostly buried in this section of the Memphis necropolis. Three major discoveries have recently been made at Sakkara, including a prime minister's tomb, a queen's pyramid, and the tomb of the son of a dynasty-founding king.

Giza: It is most famous as the location of the Giza Plateau: the site of some of the most impressive ancient monuments in the world, including the Great Sphinx, the Great Pyramid of Giza and a number of other large pyramids and temples.

Azania: The African name for South Africa.

Jeff Asmah: The Ghana Ambassador in Libya at the time I got there on my Northern tour of some African countries in February, 1988. When it became clear that airlines were not allowed to pick passengers on their flights between Tripoli and Cairo, and that I was therefore faced with the possibility of missing my appointments in Egypt, he was so dynamic and resourceful that he succeeded in "chartering" a special

747 jumbo jet for my flight from Libya to Egypt. He thus ensured that I could get there in time to fulfill engagements already lined up for me. I was the sole passenger on the aircraft.

Cheikh Anta Diop: (1923-1986) He was a Senegalese historian, anthropologist, and staunch defender of the world view known as Afrocentricity places emphasis on the human race's African origins and on the study of pre-colonial African culture and its connectedness to the rest of the peoples of the world. He has been considered one of the greatest African historians of the 20th century.

Boutros Boutros-Ghali: (1922) He is an Egyptian diplomat who was the sixth Secretary-General of the United Nations from January 1992 to December 1996. Boutros- Ghali was born in Cairo into a Coptic Christian family ("Boutros" being Coptic for "Peter") that had already provided Egypt with a prime minister (Boutros Ghali, 1846-1910).

Songhai: An ancient kingdom of Africa.

Mohammed Ali: (1942). He is a great African-American boxer and former three time World Heavyweight champion and winner of an Olympic gold medal. In 1991, Ali was crowned "Sportsman of the Century" by Sports Illustrated and the BBC. Now incapacitated, he has trained his daughter to promote boxing by women.

Anyidoho-Dey: Mr. Dey, a diplomat friend at the Ghana Embassy in Algiers, Algeria, with whose family I spent sometime during my tour of Northern African countries. While visiting with them, I teased the husband by insisting on adding his wife's maiden name, Anyidoho, to his. Anyidoho is also the name of my fellow poet, Kofi Anyidoho, her relative.

Soheir Zaki: She was one of the most famous dancers of the sixties and seventies. The late Anwar Sadat once called her "the Oum Kolthoum of dance." "As she sings with her voice, you sing with your body", he told her once. Sohair received expressions of honour from the Shah of Iran, the then Tunisian president and Gamal Abdel Nasser.

Zimbabwe Ruins: The biggest example of ancient architecture south of the Great Pyramids can be found at Great Zimbabwe, the "house of stones" built by a once great and prosperous high culture. Once thought to be the site of the legendary Mines of King Solomon, these ruins have long been the inspiration of adventurers and treasure hunters. Today, are a testimony to a thousand-year-old civilization, and also represent the proud symbol of a new country. This was the royal court of the Shona kings until the 15th century.

Thomas Sankara: (1949-1987) He was the leader of Burkina Faso (formerly known as Upper Volta) from 1983 to 1987. With a potent combination of personal charisma and social organization, his government undertook major initiatives to fight corruption and improve education, agriculture, and the status of women. His revolutionary pro- gram provoked strong opposition from traditional leaders and the country's numerically small but powerful middle class. Added to friction between radical and more conservative members of the ruling junta, these factors led to his downfall and assassination in a bloody coup d'état on October 15, 1987. His policy was oriented toward fighting corruption, promoting reforestation, averting famine, and making education and health real priorities.

Jumoke, Rosemarie Anoff: Jumoke is the daughter of Madam Rosemarie, the spouse of the Ghanaian High Commissioner to Egypt, Dr. (Brigadier) Annoff. I was their privileged guest during my week's stay in Cairo, in February, 1988.

Farouk Hosni: (Born 1938 in Alexandria, Egypt) He is an Egyptian abstract painter who was appointed in 1987 to the position of Minister of Culture, which he still holds. It is said that he has graciously refused to receive a salary for his job as Minister of Culture. In November 2006, Farouk Hosni sparked controversy among many religious Muslims, particularly the clergy, after stating publicly that the traditional Muslim veil for women, the hijab, "is a step backward for Egyptian women". In an interview published in November 2006, Hosni said that "women with their beautiful hair are like flowers and should not be covered up" and that "religion today is linked only to appearances, while every woman's veil should be inside her, not outside." Hosni remains in his job and has explained that he didn't call for stripping women of their veil, but that the veil style coming from the Arabian Peninsula (the Arab countries of the Persian Gulf) is not appropriate for Egyptian women.

Al-Azhar: The foundation of the Mosque was laid in (971 A.D). It was built in two years nearly on 988 A.D. It became a university which taught different subjects, as well as religious & other subjects. It was named Al-Azhar in honour of "Fatimah Azahraa," the prophet Muhammad's daughter.

The Rosetta Stone: The Rosetta Stone is a Ptolemaic era stele inscribed with the same passage of writing in two Egyptian language scripts (hieroglyphic and demotic) and in classical Greek. It was created in 196 BC, discovered by the French in 1799 at Rosetta, a harbour on the Mediterranean coast in Egypt, and translated in 1822 by the Frenchman, Jean-Francois Champollion. Comparative translations of the stone assisted in understanding many previously undecipherable example of hieroglyphic writing. The text of the Rosetta Stone is a decree from Ptolemy V, describing the repealing of various taxes and instructions to erect statues in temples. Weighing approximately 760 kg (1,676 pounds), it was originally thought to be granite or basalt but is currently described as granodiorite and is dark grey-pinkish. The Stone has been kept at the British Museum in London since 1802. The Rosetta Stone is a well-known example from a series of decrees, the Ptolemaic Decrees, issued by the Hellenistic Ptolemaic dynasty, which ruled Egypt from 205 BC to 30 BC. Those were the Decrees of Canopus by Ptolemy III, The Memphis Stele) by Ptolemy IV, and the Rosetta Stone decree by Ptolemy V. After Napoleon's Decrees were erected in several temple courtyards, as the decrees specified. The decree of the Rosetta Stone is also on the Stele of Noubarya and in the text engraved in the Temple of Philae. The Stele of Noubaya was found in the early 1880s, and was used to complete the lines missing from the Rosetta Stone. The French Army engineer, Captain Pierre-Francois Bouchard, discovered the stone on July 15, 1799, while guiding construction work at Fort Julien near the Egyptian port city of Rosetta (now Rashid). Scholars carried the Stone from Cairo to Alexandria alongside the troops of de Menou. The French troops in Cairo capitulated on June 22, and in Alexandria on August 30.

Nkrumah: (1907-1972) A staunch Pan-Africanist who founded the Convention People's Party (C.P.P.) and led his country to attain independence from the British. Having won an election while a political prisoner, he was released on February 12, 1951, and tasked, as Leader of Government Business to form a Government. He was also the first Prime Minister in 1957 and the first President in 1960 of Ghana. He championed the cause of African Unity through the Organisation of African Unity (OAU) and is famous for the manifesto assertion of the African liberation struggle: "The independence of Ghana is meaningless unless it is linked with the total liberation of the African continent". He campaigned and fought for the unification of the African people. In February, 1966, while he was away on a state visit to Vietnam, his government was overthrown in a military coup. Nkrumah, today, is still one of the most highly regarded leaders in African history. He was voted Africa's man of the millennium by listeners to the BBC World Service in 2000.

Gamal Abdel Nassar: (1919-1970) He is seen as one of the most important political figures in the recent history of the Middle East. Widely held as a symbol of Arab dignity and freedom, he was also a major crusader alongside hs brother-colleague, Kwame Nkrumah, for the achievement of the aspirations of the African people.

Tut-ankh-a-men: It was a 14th century B.C. King of Egypt, of the 18th dynasty. His tomb was discovered in 1927. In his book ("The Life And Death of A Pharoah) – Tutankhamen" published in 1963) Christiane Desroches- Noblecourt relates how, after Lord Carnarvon, the man who subsidized the digging up of Tutankhamen's tomb, died people then "recalled inscriptions dating back to earliest times, threatening the worst to the living who come to violate the tombs. Clearly Lord Carnarvon had broken the powerful law which forbade the disturbance of the kingdom of the dead. The angry shade had struck and Lord Carnarvon was condemned. "Then after leaving the tomb, Georges Benedite, head of the Department of Egyptian Antiquities at the Louvre, died of a stroke brought on by the stifling heat of the valley of the kings. His death was followed by that of another member of the team, Arthur C. Mace, Assistant Keeper of the Department of Egyptian Antiquities at the Metropolitan Museum of Art in New York. "From time to time the revenge of Tutankhamen shares the front page of the popular press with the Lock Ness Monster. The ghost of a long-dead pharaoh torments some sensitive collector or appears to him in a terrifying form." In 1923, Lord Carnarvon, as related by his son to Desroches-Noblecourt, visited the valley of the Kings in Upper Egypt daily. "In March he was bitten by a mosquito; the bite turned septic, and spread rapidly, he decided that he would return to Cairo" for better treatment, to which the infection yielded, but towards the end of March he contracted pneumonia. His son, Lord Porchester summoned urgently from army service in India "reaching the continental Hotel in Cairo just a few hours before his father died there at five minutes to two on the morning of April 5, 1923, without having recognized his son. At this precise moment the two ["curious"] incidents referred to earlier occurred. In Cairo, all the lights in the hotel went out and remained out for some time. The next day, the new Earl, Field Marshal Lord Allenby on a formal visit to the High Commissioner, learned that every single light in the city had also gone out. Lord Allenby asked the English engineer in charge of the electricity service the cause of this strange power failure but received no satisfactory technical explanation. The other incident concerns the dog which Lord Porchester had left in his father's care when he sailed for India, and which had grown so fond of its new master that it had kept on pining in his absence. The very morning of Lord Carnoarvon's death in Egypt, the animal left in England also howled inconsolably, and died." On February 8, 1972, the "Daily Graphic" carried the following news item: "Fear of the Pharoah's Curse has been revived in Cairo with the death of the Egyptian official involved in the shipment of the Tutankhamen treasures to London. "Many people connected with the discovery of Tutankhamen's tomb just 50 years ago have died in similar mysterious circumstances. "The death from cerebral haemorrage of Dr. Gamel Mehrez, Director-General of the Egyptian Antiquities Department, a few days ago, added to the macabre aura surrounding the relics-soon to go on show in London."

Akhenaten: (Meaning He who is beneficial to the Aten). First known as Amenhotep IV (sometimes read as Amenophis IV and meaning Amun is Satisfied) before his sixth year, he was a Pharaoh of the Eighteenth dynasty of Egypt, especially notable for single-handedly restructuring the Egyptian religion to monotheistically worship the Aten. Akhenaten's chief wife was Nefertiti, who has been made famous by her exquisitely painted bust in the Altes Museum of Berlin.

La ila illala: "There is no God, but God" (Arabic).

Table Mountain: It is a flat-topped mountain forming a prominent landmark overlooking the city of Cape Town in South Africa. The flat top of the mountain is often covered by cloud spilling over the top to form the "table cloth".

THE BOND OATH OF UBUNTU

Ubuntu: A South African term which denotes humanness: "I am because you are!"

Battle of Adowa: The battle of Adowa (also known as Adwa or sometimes by the Italian name Adua) was fought on 1 March 1896 between Ethiopia and Italy near the town of Adwa, Ethiopia, in Tigray. It was the climatic battle of the First Italo-Abyssinian War. As the twentieth century approached, Africa had been carved up between the various European powers, with the exception of the tiny republic of Liberia on the west coast of the continent and the ancient, newly landlocked kingdom of Ethiopia in the strategic Horn of Africa. Italy, a relatively newcomer to the colonial scramble for Africa, having been left with only two impoverished territories on the Horn, Eritrea and Somalia, sought to increase its influence by conquering Ethiopia and creating a land bridge between its two territories. Italy and Ethiopia faced-off in the First Italo-Abyssinian War, with the two armies at a standoff in Tigray. The remaining two brigades under Baratieri himself were outflanked and destroyed piecemeal on the slopes of Mount Belah. By noon, the survivors of the Italian army were in full retreat and the battle was over. In their flight to Eritrea, the Italians left behind all of their artillery and 11,000 rifles, as well as most of their transport. As Paul B. Henze notes, "Baratieri's army had been completely annihilated while Menelik's was intact as a fighting force and gained thousands of rifles and a great deal of equipment from the fleeing Italians. However 800 captured askaris, regarded as traitors by the Ethiopians, had their right hands and left feet amputated. As a direct result of the battle, Italy signed the Treaty of Addis Ababa, recognizing Ethiopia as an independent state. "The confrontation between Italy and Ethiopia at Adwa was a fundamental turning point in Ethiopian history," writes Henze, "in Lawyers and Lawyers of Time: A History of Ethiopia," (2000) who compares this victory to Japan's naval victory over Russia at Tsushima. "Though apparent to very few historians at the time, these defeats were the beginning of the decline of Europe as the center of world politics. On a similar note, the Ethiopian historian Bahru Zewde observed that "few events in the modern period have brought Ethiopia to the attention of the world as has the victory at Adwa." This defeat of a colonial power and the ensuing recognition of African sovereignty became rallying points for later African nationalists during their struggle for decolonization.

Timbuktooyan: See Timbuktoo.

Tutankamenic: See Tutankhamen.

Mmenson: An orchestra of seven elephant tusk horns used on state occasions (festivals, funerals) to relate history; it is used as part of the equipment behind the chief (Asantehene, Denkirahene, Mamponghene and Kibihene).

Nefertiti: Nefertiti (the beauty that has come) was the Great Royal Wife (or chief consort/wife) of the Egyptian Pharaoh Amenhotep IV (later Akhenaten), and the mother in law and probable stepmother of the Pharaoh, Tutankhamun. She may have also ruled in her own right under the name Nefernefeuaten-Nefertiti (meaning, the Aten is radiant of radiance because the Beautiful one has arrived) briefly after her husband's death and before the accession of Tutankhamun. Her name roughly translates to "the beautiful (or perfect) woman has come". She also shares her name with a type of elongated gold bead, called nefer, that she was often portrayed as wearing. She was made famous by her bust, now in Berlin's Altes Museum.

Kilimanjaro: It is the highest mountain in East Africa noted earlier for its volume eruptions.

Obintin and Obonu: These are musical instruments of the Ga people (of Ghana) which are associated with royalty.

Mantse Tackie Tawia I: He was a famous king who reigned over the Ga State from 1862 to 1902. He was noted for his forward-looking administrative genius, martial skills, intrepidity and mysterious powers. He fought many wars and helped the people of Ada to subjugate their neighbouring Ewes, thereby curbing their incursions into Ada territory. He brought the captives of war from Ada, when the Adas vanquished the Ewes, to establish the suburb Avenor in Accra. Owing to his ardent commercial interest, he travelled widely and established close ties with many of his neighbours. Through his instrumentality, the Nelsons came from Brazil to live in Accra. They were famous for the art of masonary. It was during the reign of Mantse Tackie Tawia I reign that the Bank of British West Africa (now Standard Chartered Bank Ghana Ltd) and Holy Trinity were established. So opposed was he to what he considered obnoxious colonial rules that he was exiled to the Elmina castle, but returned after a short while with an ovation to resume his rule. He not only introduced street lights but also improved the sanitation in Accra considerably. The colonial government was so impressed by his progressive rule of Accra that the capital of the Gold Coast was transferred from Cape Coast to Accra in 1876. Many were the chiefs from Southern Ghana who came to mourn him when he passed away in 1902. Now an overpass in Accra has been named after him and his statue can be found behind the Presbyterian church offices.

Fianarantsoa: It is the capital city of the Fianarantsoa Province of southeastern Madagascar, and has a population of 144,225 (2001 census). Fianarantsoa is a Malagasy expression meaning "Good education".

Altamira Caves: A cave in Northern Spain, noted for Old Stone Age wall drawings.

Great Zimbabwe: It is the name given to the remains of stone, sometimes referred to as the Great Zimbabwe Ruins, of an ancient Southern African city, located at 20 16'S 30 54'E in present-day Zimbabwe which was once the centre of a vast empire known as the Munhumutapa Empire (also called Monomotapa or Mwene Mutapa Empire). This empire ruled the territory now falling within the modern states of Zimbabwe (which took its name from this city) and Mozambique. Great Zimbabwe is modern Zimbabwe's national shrine, where the Zimbabwe Bird (a national symbol of Zimbabwe) was found. It is currently an archaeological site. Great Zimbabwe, or "houses of stone", is the name given to hundreds of great stone ruins spread out over a 200 square mile area within the modern day country of Zimbabwe, which itself is named after the ruins.

Victoria Falls: or **Mosi-oa-Tunya** are situated on the Zambezi River, on the border between Zambia and Zimbabwe, (17°55?24.05?S, 25°51?22.32?E) and are roughly 1.7 km (1 mile) wide and 128 m (420 ft) high. They are considered a remarkable spectacle because of the peculiar narrow slot-like chasm into which the water falls, so one can view the falls face-on. David Livingstone, a Scottish explorer, visited the falls in 1855 and renamed them after Queen Victoria, though they were known locally as Mosi-oa-Tunya, the "smoke that thunders".

Abu Simbel: It is an archaeological site comprising two massive rock temples in southern Egypt on the western bank of Lake Nasser about 290 km southwest of Aswan. It is part of the UNESCO World Heritage Site known as the "Nubian Monuments" which run from Abu Simbel downriver to Philae (near Aswan). The twin temples were originally carved out of the mountainside during the reign of Pharaoh Ramesses II in the 13th century BC, as a lasting monument to himself and his queen Nefertari, to commorate his alleged victory at the Battle of Kadesh, and to intimidate his Nubian neighbours.

Akosombo Dam: It is a hydroelectric dam in southeastern Ghana. The dam created the largest man-made lake in the world, known as the Lake Volta. The dam provides electricity to Ghana and the surrounding West African countries including Togo and Benin.

Abyssinia: The Abyssinia Crisis was a pre-WW2 diplomatic crisis originating in the conflict between Italy and Ethiopia (then called Abyssinia by the British). Its effects were to undermine the credibility of the League of Nations and to encourage Italy to ally with Germany. Both Italy and Ethiopia were members of the League of Nations, which had rules forbidding aggression. After their border clash at Walwal in 1934, Ethiopia appealed to the League for arbitration, but the response was dull and sluggish. There was little international protest to Mussolini when he then sent large numbers of troops to Eritrea and Italian Somaliland, two colonies of Italy that bordered Ethiopia on the North and Southeast respectively. Even actions such as the use of chemical weapons and the massacre of civilians did little to change the League's passive approach to the situation. In December 1935 Samuel Hoare of Britain and Pierre Laval of France proposed the secret Hoare- Laval Plan which would end the war but allowed Italy to control large areas of Ethiopia. Mussolini agreed to the plan, but it caused an outcry in Britain and France when the plan was leaked to the media. Hoare and Laval were accused of betraying the Abyssinians, and both resigned. The plan was dropped, but the perception spread that Britain and France were not serious about the principles of the League. After the plan was dropped, the war continued and Mussolini turned to Adolf Hitler for alliance. Soon following the Italian capture of the capital, Addis Ababa, and merging Ethiopia with its other colonies (creating Italian East Africa), all sanctions placed by the League were dropped.

A CONCERTO FOR THE BLACK SATELLITES: IN THE STOOLROOM OF THE SOUL

Jorn Utzon: He was the Danish architect whose groundbreaking design for the Sydney Opera House won the top prize in an international competition. The **Sydney Opera House** is located in Sydney, Australia. It is one of the most distinctive and famous 20th century buildings, and one of the most famous performing arts venues in the world. Situated on Bennelong Point in Sydney Harbour, with parkland to its south and close to the equally famous Sydney Harbour Bridge, the building and its surroundings form an iconic Australian image. The Sydney Opera House is a modern design, with a series of large precast concrete 'shells', each taken from the same hemisphere, forming the roofs of the structure. The roofs of the House are covered with 1.056 million glossy white and matte cream Swedish-made tiles, though from a distance the tiles look only white. Despite their self-cleaning nature, they are still subject to periodic maintenance and replacement. The basic design announced in 1957 was the one submitted by Jørn Utzon, a Danish architect. Eero Saarinen, a Finnish-American architect and product designer, served on the jury for the Sydney Opera House commission and was crucial in the selection of the design by Jørn Utzon. Utzon arrived in Sydney in 1957 to help supervise the project. The shells of the competition entry were originally of undefined geometry, but early in the design process the "shells" were perceived as a series of parabolas supported by precast concrete ribs. However, engineers Ove Arup and partners were unable to find an acceptable solution to constructing them. They had to find a way in which to economically construct the shells from precast concrete, because the framework for using in-situ concrete would have been prohibitively expensive. From 1957 to 1963 the design team went through at least twelve different iterations of the form of the shells (including schemes with parabolas, circular ribs and ellipsoids) before a workable solution was completed. The design work on the shells involved one of the earliest uses of computers in structural analysis in order to understand the complex forces the shells would be subject to. Over several years Utzon gradually made major changes in his original concept designs and gradually developed a way to construct the large shells that cover the two halls, replacing the original elliptical shells with a design based on complex sections of a sphere. Jorn Utzon was born in Copenhagen as the son of a naval engineer, and grew up in Denmark. In 1957 he unexpectedly won the competition for a new opera house in Sydney, Australia, despite the fact that it was his first non-domestic design and his entry did not meet the contest criteria because the designs he submitted were little better than preliminary drawings. Although Utzon had spectacular plans for the interior of these halls, he was unable to realise this part of his design. In mid-1965 the state Liberal government of Robert Askin was elected and Utzon soon found himself in conflict with the new Minister of Works, Davis Hughes. Attempting to rein in the escalating cost of the project, Hughes began questioning Utzon's designs, schedules and cost estimates, and he eventually stopped the payments to Utzon, who was forced to resign as chief architect in

February 1966. He secretly left the country days later, never to return. In an article in the "Harvard Design Magazine" in 2005, professor Bent Flyvbjerg argues that Utzon fell victim to a politically lowballed construction budget, which eventually resulted in a cost overrun of 1,400 percent. The overrun and the scandal it created kept Utzon from building more masterpieces. This, according to Flyvbjerg, is the real cost of the Sydney Opera House.During the construction of the Opera House, a number of lunchtime performances were arranged for the workers, with Paul Robeson the first artist to perform at the (unfinished) Opera House in 1960.The Sydney Opera House was finally completed, and opened in 1973 by Queen Elizabeth II, and is one of the world's most recognizable buildings.In March 2003, Utzon was awarded an honorary doctorate degree for his work on the opera house by the University of Sydney. Utzon's son accepted the award on his behalf as he himself was too ill to travel to Australia. Utzon has also been awarded the Order of Australia and the Keys to the City Of Sydney. He has also been involved in redesigning the Opera House, and in particular, the reception hall, following an agreement made in 2000. Also, in 2003 he received the Pritzker Prize, architecture's highest honour.In March 2006 Queen Elizabeth II opened the western colonnade addition to the building that was constructed by Utzon in the last years without his having been to Australia since 1966. His son Jan took his place at the opening ceremony instead, saying his father "is too old by now to take the long flight to Australia. But he lives and breathes the Opera House, and as its creator, he just has to close his eyes to see it."

Bennelong Point: That is the name of the place where the Sydney Opera House was built. (See Jorn Utzon, Above).

Osam Duodu: He was a member of the Black Stars technical team during the 1982 African Cup of Nations which Ghana won. He has coached all the national soccer teams in Ghana. He is now the Under 17 (Starlets) Coach.

Baba Yara: Had impressive soccer days with Asante Kotoko and the national team. The Kumasi Sports Stadium has been named after him.

Mohammed Ali: The most celebrated world heavyweight boxer. He was World Heavyweight Champion in the late 1970's and early '80's.

Kwame Saarah-Mensah: He was the Secretary of Youth and Sports in 1991 when the starlets won the World Cup in Italy.

Banini: A member of the famous starlets '91 group. He was a defender.

Dan Addo: A member of the Starlets '91 team. He was a midfielder who distributed his passes with precision.

Moro-Moro: My friend, Kwaate Nee Owoo, related to me what his mother told him: that the Moroccan wizard sleeps with one eye open!

Azuma Nelson: He was the WBC Super featherweight Champion as well as the Lightweight Champion for almost a decade. He is currently Africa's Ambassador for boxing as well as a member of the World Hall of Fame for Boxing. He has brought unparalleled fame and honour to Ghana through his prowess.

Osei Dodoo: A member of the Black Stars team that won the Cup of Nations for the fourth unprecedented time in Libya in 1982.

Otto Pfister: He was a national coach of the Black Stars.

Emmanuel Dua: A member of the Starlets '91 team. Known for his amazing control of the ball with his left foot.

Arhinful (Augustine): A member of the 1996 Olympic Games Soccer Team.

Mantse Agbonaa: It is the open space to the south adjoining the palace of the James Town Mantse (now Nii Kojo Ababio) in Accra not far from the James Town Prison, Light House and Sea View Hotel. It serves as a football park and a place for public functions.

Kuffuor (Samuel): A stalwart defender in the famous Starlets '91 team.

Akunnor (Charles): A member of the 1996 Olympic Games Soccer Team called the Black Meteors which played in Atlanta, USA.

Saka Saka Park: A popular football field in Tamale.

Roger Milla: Recently chosen by the Confederation of African Football (CAF), as the greatest African footballer over the last century. He was an influential member of the famous Cameroon national team that reached the quarterfinals at the 1990 FIFA World Cup in Italy. He was 43 years old when he featured at the World Cup.

(Isaac) Asare: A member of the Starlets '91 team. He was a defender as a left full back.

Shinkansen: It is a network of high-speed railway lines in Japan operated by Japan Railways.

Omar Mukhtar: (1862-1931) He was the leader of the resistance movement against the Italian military occupation of Libya for more than twenty years. In 1912, following the capture of Libya from the occupying Turks the previous year, Omar Mukhtar organized and devised strategies for the Libyan resistance against the Italian colonization. In October of 1911, Italian battleships reached the shores of Libya. The Italian's fleet leader, Farafelli, made a demand to the Libyans to surrender Libya to the Italians or the city would be destroyed at once. The Libyans fled, but the Italians attacked Tripoli anyway, bombing the city for three days and thereafter proclaiming the Libyan population in Tripoli to be "committed and strongly bound to Italy." The event marked the beginning of a series of battles between the Italian occupiers and the Libyan Omar Mukhtar's forces. A teacher of the Qur'an by profession, he repeatedly led his small, highly alert groups in successful attacks against the Italians, after which they would fade back into the desert terrain. In an effort to weaken the resistance movement led by Mukhtar, the Italians imprisoned Libyan men, women and children in concentration camps. By so the Italians were attempting to weaken the Libyan resistance in two ways: first, they were cutting off all food supplies so that the prisoners would starve, and secondly, they were preventing more men from joining Omar Mukhtar's forces. About 125,000 Libyans were forced into these camps, about two-thirds of whom died. Despite the imprisonment of his people, Mukhtar was determined to continue the struggle, to continue fighting for the liberation of his country and people. Mukhtar's nearly twenty year struggle came to an end when he became wounded in battle and was subsequently captured by the Italian army. The Libyan hero was treated like a prize catch by the Italians. Though in his seventies, Mukhtar was shackled with heavy chains from his waist and wrists because of the army's fear that he might escape. Mukhtar's capture was a serious blow to his people. However, his resilience had an impact on his jailors, who later said they were overwhelmed by his steadfastness. His interrogators later confessed that Mukhtar looked them in the eye and read verses of peace from the Qur'an as he was tortured and interrogated. Mukhtar was tried, convicted, and sentenced to be executed by hanging in a public place.

Amarkai (Amarteifio): A former boxer, a retired Army Major, a prominent lawyer, a sports enthusiast and patron who was a Minister of the Greater Accra Region, and later a Minister of Sports.

Ben Owu: He was the goalkeeper for the famous Starlets '91 team that won the tournament.

Sydney Cove: It is a small bay on the southern shore of Port Jackson (commonly but incorrectly called Sydney Harbour), on the coast of the state of New South Wales, Australia. It was the site chosen by Captain Arthur Phillip on 26 January 1788 (now commemorated as Australia Day) for the British penal settlement which is now the city of Sydney.

Kintampo: It is an important market town to the north of Ashanti.

Kangaroo: It is an Australian animal that moves by jumping and carries its babies in pouch which is a special pocket of skin.

Nii Odartey Lamptey: An outstanding member of the Starlets '91 team. He was voted the best player of the tournament. His dribbling skills were so unparalleled that football legend Pele admitted that Odartey was going to be next legend after him (Pele).

Mohammed Gargo: A stalwart midfielder of the Starlets '91 team whose thunderbolt shots sent shivers down the spine of opposing goalkeepers.

Naa Dzeringa: He was a Mamprusi chief in Northern Ghana who in ancient days was so security-conscious to the extent that he built a thick five-foot wall around his traditional capital, Nalerigu. He was so anxious to get this wall completed that he used substances like honey, shea butter and even the bodies of those who worked out themselves and collapsed.

Limpopo River: It is in Limpopo, the northernmost province of South Africa, on the border with Zimbabwe.

Oduduwa: According to Yoruba mythology, the world or dry land was created by Oduduwa, the son of high God Olorun whose children founded the chief Yoruba Kingdoms.

Ile Ife: Yoruba mythology asserts that this town was the cradle of mankind.

Pythagoras: A Greek philosopher and mathematician who founded a religious brotherhood which greatly influenced the development of mathematics and its application to music and astronomy. He and his followers teach that the universe is essentially a manifestation of mathematical relationships.

Naana Mensah: A friend of the poet.

Gaston Kabore: (1951) He is a Burkinabe film director. His work for the screen, focusing on his country's rural heritage, has received numerous international awards including a French Cesar. At the moment he is chairman of the Pan African Federation of scenario writers.

Ousman Sembéne: (1923) He is a Senegalese film director, producer and writer. He is considered one of the greatest authors of sub-Saharan Africa and has often been called the "Father of African film". In 1944, Sembéne was drafted into the French Army in World War II and later fought for Free French forces. After the war he returned to his home country and in 1947 participated in a long railroad strike on which he later based his seminal novel, God's Bits of Wood.

Kwesi Owusu: (1960) Dr. Kwesi Owusu, a Pan-Africanist, is the co-director of the film, AMA. A writer, music producer and film maker, he is the Chief Executive Officer of Creative Storm.

Kremlin: It is the Russian word for "fortress", "citadel", or "castle" and refers to any major fortified central complex found in historical Russian cities. This word is often used to refer to the best known one, the Moscow Kremlin, or the government that is based there. Outside Russia, the name "Kremlin" is sometimes mistakenly thought of as being Saint Basil's Cathedral because of its distinctive shape, although this is not a part of the Moscow Kremlin.

Kwaw Ansah: (1941) A distinguished African film maker from Ghana. His widely acclaimed films are "Love Brewed In An African Pot", and the prize-winning "Heritage Africa". A committed Pan Africanist, he is the Chief Executive Officer of TV Africa.

Ngugi: He is a Kenyan author, formerly working in English and now working in Gĩkũyũ. Ngugi went into self-imposed exile following his release from a Kenyan prison in 1977. His family was caught up in the Mau Mau rebellion; he lost his stepbrother, and his mother was tortured. The uncensored political message of his 1977 play Ngaahika Ndeenda (I Will Marry When I Want) provoked then Vice President Daniel arap Moi to order his arrest. While detained in the Kamiti Maximum Security Prison, he wrote the first modern novel in Gĩkũyũ., Caitaani mũtharaba-Inĩ (Devil on the Cross), on prison-issued toilet paper. His later works include Detained, his prison diary (1981), Decolonizing the Mind: The Politics of Language in African Literature (1986), an essay arguing for African writers' expression in their native languages, rather than European languages, in order to renounce lingering colonial ties and to build an authentic African literature.

Kwate Nii Owoo: (1944) A Ghanaian film maker, co-producer/director of the film, AMA, he is the head of the Media Unit of the Institute of African Studies, University of Ghana, Legon and the Executive Director of Efiri-Tete Communications and Efiri-Tete Multimedia. A Pan- Africanist.

Turkish Lips: The referee was from Turkey.

Nii Tackie Kome II: Ga Mantse (1948-1962) He contributed immensely towards the attainment of independence. "In his capacity as the Ga Mantse, he ruled against the decision of some chiefs and prominent members of society, notably, Hutton-Mills, Dr. Nanka Bruce, and Obetsebi-Lamptey, and some leading members of the United Party (UP) not to allow Dr. Kwame Nkrumah to contest the 1951 parliamentary election at Accra Central (wards 6, 7 and 8 now Odododiodoo). "When the colonial government wanted to arrest Dr. Nkrumah for declaring 'Positive Action' and was combing the whole of Accra looking for him, the late King hid him in the stool room of the Ga paramount stool against custom." (A statement to the Press on 16th February, 2007, by the Member of Parliament for Odododiodo, Jonathan Nii Tackie Komme; see "The Heritage" (Accra), 19th February, 2007, p. 6).

Okomfo Anokye: was from Awukugua and famous for commanding the Ashanti golden stool from the skies which was entrusted to his friend Osei Tutu.

Kwegyir Aggrey: (1875-1927) "The great African nationalist". He often recounted an inspirational tale about Africa to his audiences, especially the students at the Achimota College when he was on the school's staff. It is about a hunter who comes upon an eagle feeding together with chickens. The hunter lifts up the eagle and reminds it that it does not belong on the ground, among chicken but that it belongs to the skies. It should fly away into its own proper environment, the skies. The hunter throws it up into the air to fly, and it falls back to the ground. After several attempts and exhortations, he goes up a hill, sets off the eagle into the air, and it finally flies away. He likened the story of the eagle to the plight, potential and destiny of Africa. He called for racial harmony by saying that you need to play both the white and black keys of the piano to produce harmony.

THE GUILLOTINE OF TIME: FANFARE FOR THE UNCOMMON WOMAN

Aaron Copland: (1900-1990) He was an American composer of concert and film music. Instrumental in forging a distinctly American style of composition, he was widely known as "the dean of American composers." Copland's music achieved a difficult balance between modern music and American folk styles, and the open, slowly changing harmonies of many of his works are said to evoke the vast American landscape. He incorporated percussive orchestration, changing meter, polyrhythms, polychords and tone rows. Outside of composing, Copland often served as a teacher and lecturer. Although his parents never encouraged or directly exposed him to music, at the age of fifteen he had already taken an interest in the subject and aspired to be a composer. Upon his return from his studies in Paris, he decided that he wanted to write works that were "American in character" and thus he chose jazz as the American idiom. Several composers rejected the notion of writing music for the elite during the Depression, thus the common American folklore served as the basis for his work along with revival hymns, and cowboy and folk songs. Fanfare for the Common Man, perhaps Copland's most famous work, scored for brass and percussion, was written in 1942 at the request of the conductor Eugene Goossens, conductor of the Cincinnati Symphony Orchestra. It would later be used to open many Democratic National Conventions. The fanfare was also used as the main theme of the fourth movement of Copland's Third Symphony, where it first appears in a quiet, pastoral manner, then in the brassier form of the original.

Pablo Piccasso: (1880-1973) He was a famous Spanish painter and sculptor. His full name is **Pablo Diego José Francisco de Paula Juan Nepomuceno María de los Remedios Crispín Crispiniano de la Santísima Trinidad Ruizy Picasso.** One of the most recognized figures in 20th century art, he is best known as the co-founder, along with Georges Braque, of cubism. It has been estimated that Picasso produced about 13,500 paintings or designs, 100,000 prints or engravings, 34,000 book illustrations and 300 sculptures or ceramics.

George Gershwin: (1898-1937) He was an American composer who wrote most of his vocal and theatrical works in collaboration with his elder brother lyricist Ira Gershwin. In 1924, Gershwin composed his first classical work, Rhapsody in Blue for orchestra and piano. It proved to be his most popular work. Early in 1937, Gershwin began to complain of blinding headaches and a recurring impression that he was smelling burned rubber. Unbeknown to him, he had developed a brain tumor. It was in Hollywood, while working on the score of The Goldwyn Follies, that he collapsed and, on July 11, 1937, died following surgery for the tumor at the age of 38.

Enoch Mankayi Sontonga: He wrote, the song Njisu Sikelel' iAfrika, Enoch Sontonga, from the Mpinga clan, of the Xhosa nation, was born in the Eastern Cape in about 1873. It is believed that he received training as a teacher at Lovedale Institution and was then sent to a Methodist Mission school in Nancefield, near Johannesburg. He was also a choirmaster and a photographer. Sontonga died at the age of 32. on 18 April 1905. Enoch Mankayi Sontonga wrote the first verse and chorus of Njisu Sikelel' iAfrika and also composed the music in 1879. It was first sung in public in 1899 at the ordination of Rev Boweni, a Shangaan Methodist Minister. Sontonga's choir as well as other choirs sang this song around Johannesburg and Natal. This song made a strong impression on all audiences. On 8 January 1912, at the first meeting of the South African Native National Congress (SANNC), the forerunner of the African National Congress, it was immediately sung after the closing prayer. In 1925 the ANC officially adopted it as a closing anthem for its meetings. It is still the national anthem of Tanzania and Zambia and has also been sung in Zimbabwe, Namibia and South Africa for many years. In 1994 it became part of South Africa's national anthem. Over the years, several unsuccessful attempts had been made to locate Sontonga's grave in Brammfontein cemetery. On 24 September 1996, Heritage Day, the grave of Enoch Sontonga, was declared a national monument and a fitting memorial, erected on the site, was unveiled by President Nelson Mandela. At the ceremony the Order of Meritorious Service (Gold) was bestowed on Enoch Sontonga posthumously. His granddaughter, Mrs Ida Rabotape received it.

Ibrahim Adbulla: (1934) Perhaps the most gifted African musician working within the fused ancestral of African+American music, Abdullah Ibrahim, formerly known as Dollar Brand, is a pianist, composer, arranger, band leader and transformative tool.

Miriam Makeba: (1932) She is a South African singer, also known by the name Mama Afrika. She was born in Johannesburg; her mother was a Swazi sangoma and her father, who died when she was six, was a Xhosa. In 1963, after an impassioned testimony before the

United Nations Committee Against apartheid, her records were banned in South Africa and her South African citizenship and her rights to return to the country were revoked. Nelson Mandela persuaded her to return to South Africa in 1990.

Hugh Masekela: (1939) He is a South African flugelhorn and cornet player. In 1961, as part of the anti-apartheid campaign, he was exiled to the United States. In 1987, he had a hit single with "Bring Him Back Home" which became an anthem for the movement to free Nelson Mandela. After apartheid ended, Masekela returned to South Africa where he now lives.

George Bizos: Born 1982 in Greece, he is a distinguished human rights advocate who defended the nationalists fighting against apartheid in South Africa. Bizos was counsel to Trevor Huddleston of Sophiatown in the 1950s, and since then has been counsel to Nelson Mandela. He was part of the team that defended Mandela, Govan Mbeki and Walter Sisulu in the Rivonia Trial in 1963-64, in which the defendants were sentenced to life imprisonment, but spared the death penalty. He credits to himself the drafting of Mandela's famous speech spoken at the trial. He has defended Winnie Madikizela-Mandela on more than 20 occasions.

Walter Chakela: (1953) He is a South African playwright, poet, theatre, television director and the Executive Chairperson, Chakela ad Associates and the former Chief Executive Officer of the Wyndybrow Centre for the Arts in Johannesburg.

Arthur Molepo: A South African actor.

Tina Mnumzana: A South African actress.

Nkotsi Sol Plaatjie: Sol Plaatje was born on Boskop farm in the Boshof district, Orange Free State province in 1875. Being fluent in 8 languages, and with a working knowledge of several more, he then went on to work as a court interpreter and magistrate's clerk. In 1912 he became the first secretary-general of the African National Congress, recently initiated by the Rev. John Dube. His paper was renamed 'Tsala ea Batho' (Friend of the People) in 1913, he struggled to stay open, and ceased publication in 1915. A staunch opponent of the Botha government's 1913 Native Land Act (which drastically curtailed black land ownership) Plaatje formed part of a protest deputation of 5 to Britain, hoping vainly to induce a veto from a British government preoccupied with imminent war. In 1921 he founded the Brotherhood society, which concerned itself with the promotion of racial harmony. He was later to join Dr. A. Abdurahman's African Peoples Organization and to represent the African National Congress at their 1927 Pretoria conference. Besides editing and writing much for English, Afrikaans, Setswana, Xhosa and Sotho newspapers, he produced political works, and his first novel in English. 'Mhudi: An epic of South African native life a hundred years ago' (1930).

Gerard Sekoto: (1913 -1993) He is a famous black South African artist and musician, recognised as the pioneer of urban black art, social realism, and more recently as the father of South African art. Periods of residence in Sophiatown, Johannesburg, District Six, Cape Town, and Eastwood, Pretoria, produced vibrant and powerful pieces evoking both the colourful culture activity and the tensions of the townships. The paintings from this time are historical records of a now extinct way of life. All three areas were bulldozed in the fifties and sixties. In 1947 Sekoto made the momentous decision to leave the country of birth and travel to Paris-like many voluntary and involuntary exiles, he was never to return to South Africa.

Nadine Gordimer: (1923) She is a South African writer, political activist and winner of the 1991 Nobel Prize in Literature. At the age of 15, she had her first adult fiction published. Gordimer's first novel, **The Lying Days,** was published in 1953. The arrest of her best friend, Bettie du Toit, in 1960 and the Sharpeville massacre spurred Gordimer's entry into the anti-apartied movement. Therefore, she quickly became increasingly active in South African politics, and was close friends with Nelson Mandela's defense attorneys (Bram Fischer and George Bizos) during his 1962 trial. During the 1960's and 1970's, the South African government banned three of her works, along with works by other anti-apartheid writers. She hid ANC leaders in her own home to aid their escape from arrest by the government, and she has said that the proudest day of her life was when she testified at the 1986 Delmas treason trial on behalf of 22 South African anti-apartheid activists. When Mandela was released from prison in 1990, Gordimer was one of the first people he wanted to see.

Leonardo da Vinci: He is a famous 18th Century Italian artist.

Michelangelo: He is a famous 18th Century Italian artist.

Chris Hani: A freedom fighter and political activist, Tembisile Chris Hani was born in the rural village of Sabalele, in the Cofimvaba region of the former Traskei. The name Chris was adopted by him as a nom de guerre, and was in fact the real name of his brother. Hani's political involvement began in 1957 when he became a member of the African National Congress Youth League (ANCYL). His political career spanned a period of 30 years, culminating in his tragic death by an assassin's bullet in 1993. By 1987 Hani had become Chief of Staff of Umkontho, which was intensifying its struggle against the Pretoria government. On his return to South Africa in 1990, he became a member of the Politburo of the South African Communist party (SACP). Chris Hani's popularity with the masses, especially the youth, was legendary. He polled the most votes, after Nelson Mandela, in an opinion poll in November 1992, and became Secretary-General of the small but powerful SACP in 1991. On the morning of Saturday 10 April 1993, Hani was gunned down as he stepped out of his car in the driveway of his modest Dawn Park, Boksburg home. With him was his daughter, Nomakhwezi, then 15 years old. His wife, Limpho, and two other daughters, Neo (then 20 years old) and lindiwe (then 14 years old) were away at the time. More than 150,000 people attended Hani's funeral on 19 April 1993, before the first democratic elections for which he had fought so hard.

Mshenguville: It is an informal settlement in the Mofolo area of Soweto. It has been established since 1988 when a golf course was invaded by homeless people. Some 650 shacks exist in the area with approximately 4.5 people living in each unit, thus the population is nearly 3000 adults and children. As this is an "illegal" settlement, no proper facilities have been provided although water points and temporary toilets are provided on the perimeter of the settlement.

Amedeo Modigliani: (1884-1920) He was a Jewish- Italian painter and sculptor who pursued his carrier for the most part in France. Influenced by the artists in his circle of friends and associates, by a range of genres and movements, and by primitive art, Modigliani's oeuvre was nonetheless unique and idiosyncratic. He died in Paris of tubercular meningitis – exacerbated by a lifestyle of excess – at the age of 35.

Cassirer: The maiden name of Nadine Gordimer.

Rhinehold: The name of Nadine Gordimer's husband.

Trotsky: Leon Trotsky was a Russian revolutionary who served as second in command to V. I. Lenin. After the death of Lenin in 1924, Trotsky fell out with Stalin and was expelled from the Government.

Steve Biko: He was an anti-apartheid activist in South Africa in the 1960s and 1970s. A student leader, he later founded the Black Consciousness Movement which would empower and mobilize much of the urban black population. Since his death in police custody, he has been called a martyr of the anti-apartheid movement. He was famous for his slogan, "black is beautiful", which he described as meaning: "man, you are okay as you are, begin to look upon yourself as a human being".

In 1972 he was expelled from the University of Natal because of his political activities. He was banned by the apartheid regime in 1973, meaning that he was not allowed to speak to more than one person at a time nor to speak in public, and could not write publicly or speak with the media. It was also forbidden to quote anything he said, including speeches or simple conversations.

On 18 August 1977, Biko was arrested at a police roadblock under the Terrorism Act No 83 of 1967, and interrogated by the security police for twenty-two hours. It included torture and beatings resulting in a coma. He suffered a major head injury while in police custody, and was chained to a window grille for a day.

On 11 September 1977, police loaded him in the back of a Land Rover, naked and restrained in manacles, and began the 1100 km drive to Pretoria to take him to a prison with hospital facilities. He died shortly after arrival there.

The police claimed his death was the result of an extended hunger strike, but an autopsy revealed a brain hemorrhage from the massive injuries to the head, which many saw as strong evidence that he had been brutally clubbed by his captors.

Morakabe: South African poet, Morakabe Seakhoa.

Francisco Goya: (1746-1828) He was a Spanish painter and printmaker. He has been regarded both as the last of the old masters and as the first of the moderns. The subversive and subjective element in his art, as well as his bold handling of paint, provided a model for the work of later generations of artists, notably Manet and Picasso.

Golgotha: It is associated with the crucifixion of Jesus Christ.

Jabulani: Be joyful, be happy (Zulu language).

Henri Laurens: (1885-1954) He was a French sculptor and illustrator.

Henri Toulouse-Lautrec: (1864-1901) He was a French painter, printmaker, draftsman, and illustrator.

Johannes Gutenburg: (c. 1398-1468) He was a German goldsmith and inventor credited with inventing a movable type printing in Europe (circa. 1450). His major work, the Gutenberg Bible, also known as the 42-line bible, has been acclaimed for its high aesthetic and technical quality.

William Gates: (Born 1955 in Seattle, Washington) He is an American entrepreneur and the co-founder, chairman, former chief software architect, and former CEO of Microsoft, the world's largest software company. Gates is one of the best-known entrepreneurs of the personal computer revolution.

Tinabantu: "We the people" (Zulu language).

Brandenburger Tor (Brandenburg Gate): The Brandenburg Gate is the trademark of Berlin. The main entrance to the city, surrounded by the wall for thirty years, was known throughout the world as a symbol for the division of the city and for the division of the world into two power blocs. It was built as the grandest of a series of city gates constituting the passages through the customs wall encircling the city at the end of the eighteenth century. It is the only gate which survived because it constitutes the monumental termination of Unter den Linden, the renowned boulevard of linden trees which led directly to the residence of the Prussian kings until the destruction of the city castle. The entire construction and ornamentation of the gate reflect the extraordinary importance it was granted by its builders. The architect selected as the model for his design the Propylaea in Athens, the monumental entry hall of the Acropolis. Just as the Propylaea led to a shrine of the Ancient world, this gate was to represent the access to the most important city of the Prussian kingdom.

Frantz Fanon: Frantz Fanon's relatively short life yielded two potent and influential statements of anti-colonial revolutionary thought, Black Skin, White Masks (1952) and The Wretched of the Earth (1961), works which have made Fanon a prominent contributor to postcolonial studies. In 1953, Fanon became Head of the Psychiatry Department at the Blida-Joinville Hospital in Algeria, where he instituted reform in patient care and desegregated the wards. During his tenure in Blida, the war for Algerian independence broke out, and Fanon was horrified by the stories of torture his patients – both French torturers and Algerian torture victims – told him. The Algerian War consolidated Fanon's alienation from the French imperial viewpoint, and in 1956 he formally resigned his post with the French government to work for the Algerian cause. But Fanon's work for Algerian independence was not confined to writing. During his tenure as Ambassador to Ghana for the Provisional Algerian Government, he worked to establish a southern supply route for the Algerian army. Fanon died at the National Institutes of Health in Bethesda, Maryland, where he had sought treatment for his cancer, on December 6, 1961. At his request, his body was returned to Algeria and buried with honours by the Algerian National Army of Liberation.

Squattercamp: A squatter camp is any "camp" located on any property that you do not own or which you have no actual and proper permission to occupy from the true owner.

Sharpeville Massacre: The **Sharpeville massacre**, also known as the **Sharpeville shootings,** occurred on March 21, 1960, when South African police opened fire on a crowd of black protesters. The confrontation occurred in the town- ship of Sharpeville, in what is now Gauteng province. In a protest organized by the PAC on March 21, a group of between 5,000 and 7,000 people converged on the local police station, offering themselves up for arrest for not carrying their pass books. Sixty-seven people were killed, and over 180 injured. Most of those killed and injured were women and children; the photographs taken at various places in Sharpeville at the time of the massacre show no sign of any weapon which might cause the police to open fire on the protestors. The statements of Lieutenant Colonel Pienaar show that the mere gathering of blacks was taken as a provocation: "The Native mentality does not allow them to gather for a peaceful demonstration. For them to gather means violence." The uproar among blacks was immediate, and the following week saw demonstrations, protest marches, strikes, and riots around the country. On March 30, 1960, the government declared a state of emergency, detaining more than 18,000 people.

FANFARE FOR CABRAL

Chaka the Zulu: Chaka, "Great Zulu warrior", "The Black Napoleon", "Absolute ruler and tyrant." These were the titles and characteristics used when describing Chaka. He was a strong leader and military innovator. Chaka is noted for revolutionizing l9th Century Bantu warfare. He was a man with great power and the heart of a tiger.

Chaka had no rifles, and different from Napoleon, used hand-to-hand war tactics. Chaka was born in 1786, the son of Senzangakona, a Zulu Chief and his mother Nandi. Chaka built the Zulu tribe into a powerful nation of more than one million, and united all the tribes in South Africa against colonial rule.

Eduardo Mondlane: Eduardo Chivambo Mondlane (1920- 1969) is regarded as the father of Mozambican independence. The fourth of 16 sons of a chieftain of the Bantuspeaking Tsonga tribe, Mondlane was born in Portuguese East Africa in 1920. He worked as a shepherd until the age of 12. In 1962, Mondlane was elected president of the newly formed Mozambican Liberation Front (Frente de Libertação de Moçambique or FRELIMO). FRELIMO began a guerilla war in 1964 to obtain Mozambique's independence from Portugal. In 1969, a bomb was planted in a book then sent to him at the FRELIMO secretariat. It exploded, killing him. It was discovered that the Portuguese branch of Gladio had murdered him. In 1975, Portugal and FRELIMO negotiated Mozambique's independence.

Murtala Mohammed: (1938-1976) A former Head of State of Nigeria, who came to power in 1975, and was killed on Friday 13th, 1976. He was a true African committed to the liberation of Africa. He made the famous speech in November, 1976 that Africa had come of age. He supported the liberation struggle in South Africa, and nationalized the Shell BP either in November or December, 1975. He was overthrown and killed for his patriotic and anti-imperialist stand on Africa and Africans.

Sojourner Truth: (c. 1797-1883) was the self-given name, from 1843, of Isabella Baumfree, an American abolitionist. Sojourner Truth was born into slavery in Swartekill, New York. Her most famous speech, which became known as Ain't I a Woman?, was delivered in 1851 at the Ohio Women's Rights Convention in Akron, Ohio. **Isabella Baumfree** was born around the year 1797. She was born into slavery on the Hardenbergh estate in Swartekill, New York. Her parents were James and Betsy Baumfree, slaves of Colonel Hardenbergh. She was one of thirteen children. She spoke only Dutch until she was sold. Ownership of the family slaves passed to the Colonel's son, Charles Hardenbergh, at the death of the colonel. In 1806 Isabella was sold to John Neely, along with a herd of sheep, near Kingston, New York for $100. Then she was sold in 1808, for $105, to Martinus Schryver of Kingston, New York, where she stayed for 18 months. She was sold again in 1810, for $175, to John Dumont of New Paltz, New York. Isabella suffered many hardships at the hands of Mrs. Dumont, whom Isabella later described as cruel and harsh.

Malcolm X: (1925-1965) was a Black Muslim Minister and National Spokesman for the Nation of Islam. During his life, Malcolm became one of the most prominent black nationalist leaders in the United States. He ultimately rose to become a world-renowned African American/Pan- Africanist and human rights activist. Following a pilgrimage to Mecca in 1964, Malcolm became a Sunni Muslim. Less than a year later he was assassinated in Washington.

Rev. Martin Luther King, Jnr.: (1929-1968) A famous leader of the American civil rights movement, a distinguished theologian and public speaker who championed the cause of the Black American for which he was assassinated on April 4, 1968. He has become illustrious in American history.

Che Guevara: (1928-1967) commonly known as **Che Guevara** or **El Che,** was an Argentine-born Marxist revolutionary, political figure, and leader of Cuban and internationalist guerrillas. Guevara joined Fidel Castro's revolutionary 26th of July Movement, which seized power in Cuba in 1959. He was captured in Bolivia and was summarily executed by the Bolivian Army on October 9, 1967. After his death, Guevara became an icon of socialist revolutionary movements worldwide.

Mahatma Ghandi: (1869-1948) He was a major political and spiritual leader of India and the Indian independence movement. In India, he is recognized as the Father of the Nation. October 2nd, his birthday, is each year commemorated as Gandhi Jayanti, and is a national holiday. He was the pioneer of Satyagraha—the resistance of tyranny through mass civil disobedience, firmly founded upon ahimsa or total non—violence-which led India to independence and inspired movements for civil rights and freedom across the world. Gandhi is popularly known in India and across the world as **Mahatma Gandhi.**

"See me Lakayana with my spear": This is a famous line from one of the stories in the Oxford English Reader used in most schools of the British Colonies.

Amílcar Cabral: (1924-1973) He was an African agronomic engineer, writer and nationalist politician. Cabral led African nationalism movements in Guinea-Bissau and the Cape Verde Islands and led

Guinea-Bissau's independence movement. He was assassinated in 1973, just months before Guinea-Bissau gained independence.

Pistalet i snoval solgal: (Russian language): "The pistol again has lied".

Taflatse: An expression used before an unpleasant or uncouth expression that one has to use usually before the elders. It is an expression of humility on the part of the speaker and a show of respect to the elders. It is used before the uttering of a proverb, whose wisdom is said to belong to the elders.

Vasco da Gamma: (c. 1469-1524) He was a Portuguese explorer, one of the most successful in the European Age of Discovery, and the first person to sail directly from Europe to India.

António de Spínola: (1910-1996) was a Portuguese soldier and politician. Spinola served in several positions in Portugal's rebellious colonies in Africa. In 1961 Spínola was sent to Angola, and in 1968 Spinola was appointed as the governor of Portuguese Guinea and Chief of the Army Forces there. As a conservative he disliked the leftist direction of the revolution and tried to avoid the independence of the colonies.

Guinea Bissau: Officially the **Republic of Guinea-Bissau,** is a country in western Africa, and one of the smallest nations in continental Africa. Formerly the Portuguese colony of Portuguese Guinea.

Mozambique: The Republic of Mozambique is a country in southern Africa, bordered by Swaziland, Tanzania, Malawi, Zambia and Zimbabwe.

Angola: Is a country in south-central Africa bordering Namibia, Democratic Republic of the Congo, and Zambia, and with a west coast along the Atlantic Ocean.

Siphiwe Nyanda: General **Siphiwe Nyanda** SSA SBS CSL DMG MMS MMM (born 1950) was a South African military commander. He joined Umkhonto weSizwe (MK), the military wing of the African National Congress, in 1974, and served as a field commander during the liberation struggle against the South African government in the 1980s. He was appointed MK Chief of Staff in 1992, and served on the Transitional Executive Council which oversaw the change of government in 1994.

Soweto: Is an urban area in the City of Johannesburg, in Gauteng, South Africa. Its name is an English syllabic abbreviation, short for

South Western Townships. Soweto came to the world's attention on June 16, 1976 with the Soweto Riots, when mass protests erupted over the government's policy to enforce education in Afrikaans rather than English. Police opened fire in Orlando West on 10,000 students marching from Naledi High School to Orlando Stadium, and in the events that unfolded, 566 people died.

WATU WAZURI

Watu Wazari: Beautiful people (Swahili).

Stevie Wonder: (born on 1950), A remarkable musical talent, is an African American singer, songwriter, record producer, musician, and social activist. Blind from infancy. He has become one of the most successful and well-known artist in the world. A multi-instrumentalist, Wonder plays the drums, congas, bass guitar, organ, harmonica and most famously the piano.

Waumbaji: Creators (Swahili).

Rhododendrons in donkeydom: Rhododendrons (flowers) in the Kingdom of donkeys.

Aluta Continua: The struggle still continues! (Spanish).

Ludwig van Beethoven: (1770-1827) He was a German composer. He is generally regarded as one of the greatest composers in the history of music. While primarily known today as a composer, he was also a celebrated pianist and conductor, and an accomplished violinist. In his late twenties he began to lose his hearing gradually, and yet he continued to produce notable masterpieces throughout his life, even when his deafness was almost total.

Ray Charles: (1930-2004) was a pioneering American pianist and soul musician who shaped the sound of rhythm and blues. When Ray was five, his four-year-old brother George drowned in an outside washing tub. Not long after this event, Ray began to go blind, becoming totally blind by the age of seven. Charles never knew exactly why he lost his sight, though there are sources which suggest Ray's blindness was due to glaucoma. He attended school at the St. Augustine School for the Deaf and the Blind in St. Augustine, Florida. He also learned how to write music and play various musical instruments. While he was there, his mother died. His father died two years later.

Tinkongkong: The sound of the gongong played to call together a clan to order on special occasions such as the death of an elder or nobleman in the clan or the celebration of any festival in the clan among the Gas. It is from the word Tikro – a Twi word, meaning: one head, symbolising unity.

EVENSONG AT SOWETO

Ayawaso: The place where Ayite, the second Ga Mantse built the ancient capital town of the Gas, by the Okai Koi hill, on the old Nsawam road, 11 kilometres from Accra. The Ga people arrived there in 1275 from Mesopotamia or Babylon – Ayawaso is an Awutu (Obutu) word – taken from the word: Ayeekoo; so is a hill (s. Tserepong word of the Larteh people and also of Krachi).

A Kpele song says: Game nuu ga – which means that both the Gas and the Tserepongs know the Tserepong and Ga languages. The Gas called that place Kpla Gong – taken from the word Kpla: (Ni akpla aahu le, ni abawa gon le no meaning: After they had moved (trekked) and moved on, then they got here (stopping on the hill).

Ofruntum: A large rubber tree – funtumia elastica. An Akan saying goes thus: Ofruntum wuo sane mmatatwene, meaning: Ofruntum's death affects (the innocent) mmatatwene (climber). Its symbolism in the context of this poem is the fact that the fate of the climber is linked to that of the ofruntum.

Soweto: A town in the South Africa.

Nye hea awo: (Awo is God) Embrace God – and gain blessings. [The Passover: The angel of God will pass over you this night – so all should stay indoors]. Nye hea awo means "Peace be unto you…" This is chanted on the Friday preceding the Saturday for the Homowo festival. (No one on that night is allowed out for the king and his men will be passing round, blessing the town (see Reindorf 112).

"Nikosi sikelelai afrika": God bless Africa (Zulu).

Ana nme anaa te: An oath of the Ga people: in other words: pool your resources, we are in a dilemma.

"Sane ko mii domi ee…": I am deeply pained (Ga).

"Afrika le okropong ni": Africa is an eagle (Ga).

"Agro Beye yie…": The beginning forecasts the end (Twi).

Ayawaso: The place where Ayite, the second Ga Mantse built the ancient capital town of the Gas, by the Okai Koi hill, on the old

Nsawam road, 11 miles from Accra. The Ga people arrived there in 1275 from Mesopotamia or Babylon – Ayawaso is an Awutu (Obutu) word – taken from the word: Ayeekoo; so is a hill (s. Tserepong word of the Larteh people and also of Krachi).

A Kpele song says: Game nuu ga – which means that both the Gas and the Tserepongs know the Tserepong and Ga languages. The Gas called that place Kpla Gong – taken from the word Kpla: (Ni akpla aahu le, ni abawa gon le no meaning: After they had moved (trekked) and moved on, then they got here (stopping on the hill). But the Owutu people call it Ayawaso. (All the Larteh, Tserepong, Awutu and Guan people speak one language). There is a town in Nuba (Nubia) South of Egypt called Mashi and hence Ga Mashi. Mashi means origin of the country. (Cosmopolitan).

Ofruntum: A large rubber tree – funtumia elastica.

An Akan saying goes thus: Ofruntum wuo sane mmatatwene, meaning: Ofruntum's death affects (the innocent) mmatatwene (climber). Its symbolism in the context of this poem is the fact that the fate of the climber is linked to that of the ofruntum.

Asante Kotoko: It is one of the most formidable football teams in Ghana. It has a Kumasi base and its chairman is the Asantehene.

MANDELA THE SPEAR

James Fort: It was one of the earliest European forts built in Accra. Now it houses the James Town prison. This was the very prison in which Kwame Nkrumah was incarcerated during the independence struggle. It was therefore from here that he had to emerge triumphant on 12 February, 1951, after the general election results declared him the winner of the seat in the Accra Central constituency. Thousands of people were outside the prison gate awaiting his release to hail and receive him. The following day, he was invited by the Governor to form a government.

Sakumo: It is a lagoon at Tema.

Larabanga: It is a town in north western Ghana. It is known for its mud-built whitewashed Sahelian mosque, said to date from 1421 at the height of the trans-Saharan trade. It is reputed to be Ghana's oldest mosque and houses a copy of the Qur'an almost as old. The town is also known for its Mystic Stone, for its patterned vernacular architecture and as the entrance to the Mole National Park.

Ogun: A Yoruba god.

Niyi Osundare: (1947) A distinguished and prolific Nigerian poet, dramatist and literary critic. Osundare is renowned for his commitment to socially relevant art and artistic activism. Osundare believes that there is no choice for the African poet but to be political.

Femi Osofisan: (1946) A distinguished and prolific Nigerian critic, poet, actor and playwright whose work is preoccupied with the themes of injustice and political corruption.

Festus Iyayi: A distinguished Nigerian novelist and rights activist; an apostle of good governance and social justice, Iyayi took on the military headlong and fearlessly. The former radical president of the Academic Staff Union of Universities (ASUU), at different times was battered, bloodied and incarcerated. But the award-winning author of Heroes, Violence, Awaiting Court Martial, and Contract remained unbowed and uncowered. "I was stripped naked and asked to pack faeces with my bare hands. The police there then asked the inmates to beat me up", Prof. Iyayi recalls. The conscience and principles of the Head of Department of Business Administration of the University of Benin are allergic to a visionless ruling class.

Ngorongoro Crater: Ngorongoro Crater Lodge is perched on the edge of the world-famous Ngorongoro Crater at the eastern edge of the Serengeti in northern Tanzania. It lies within the Ngorongoro Conservation Area, which covers more than 8 000 square kilometres (3 100 square miles) of pristine African wilderness.

Lalibela: is a town in northern Ethiopia. Lalibela is one of Ethiopia's holiest cities, second only to Aksum. This rural town is known around the world for its monolithic churches which play an important part in the history of rock-cut architecture. Though the dating of the churches is not well established, most are thought to have been built during the reign of Lalibela, namely during the 12th and 13th centuries. There are 12 churches, assembled in four groups.

Moshoeshoe: (1786-1870) It is the name of the man who originated the union of several Bechuana tribes from which arose the Basuto people at the beginning of the 19th Century. For his wisdom, foresight and clever diplomatic ability, British historians called him the "African Bismarck" (Endre Sik.)

Dingaan: (ca. 1795-1840) He was a Zulu chief who became king in 1828. He came to power after assassinating his half-brother Shaka with the help of another brother, Umthlangana, as well as Shaka's advisor Mbopa.

Patrice Lumumba: (1925-1961) He was an African anticolonial leader and the first legally elected Prime Minister of the Democratic Republic of the Congo after he helped to win its independence from Belgium in June 1960. Only ten weeks later, Lumumba's government was deposed in a coup during the Congo Crisis. He was subsequently imprisoned and assassinated under controversial circumstances. Patrice Lumumba continues to serve as a significant inspirational figure in the Congo as well as throughout Africa.

Samora Machel: (1933-1986) He was President of Mozambique from 1975 until he died eleven years later, when his presidential aircraft crashed in a mountainous terrain where the borders of Mozambique, Swaziland and South Africa converge.

Steve Biko: (1946-1977) He was a noted nonviolent antiapartheid activist in South Africa in the 1960s. He helped found the South African Students' Organization (SASO) in 1968, and was elected its first president. The SASO evolved into the influential Black Consciousness Movement (BCM). He was banned during the height of apartheid in March 1973. In spite of the repression of the apartheid government, Biko and the BCM played a significant role in organizing the protests which culminated in the Soweto Uprising of 16 June 1976. On 18 August 1977, Biko was arrested at a police roadblock under the Terrorism Act No 83 of 1967. He suffered a major head injury while in police custody, and was chained to a window grille for a full day. On 11 September 1977 police loaded him into the back of a car and began the 740-mile drive to Pretoria. He died shortly after arrival at the Pretoria prison. The police claimed his death was the result of an extended hunger strike. He was found to have massive injuries to the head, which many saw as strong evidence that he had been brutally clubbed by his captors.

MANDELA THE AFRICAN WARRIOR

Abelenkpe: It is one of the many suburbs in Accra, Ghana; it also means "Corn is what I am chewing" (the Ga language).

Nketie nta: (the Ga language), means "Groundnuts is what I am chewing".

Oyibi: is a small township some 20 miles to the east of Accra and 5 miles to Dodowa. Now a housing estate is developing there. The Valley View University is sited there. The land belongs to the Nungua Stool. Nungua is a suburb of Accra on the eastern coast.

Madiba: (In South Africa, "Madiba" is an affectionate nickname for President Nelson Mandela).

Hendrick Witbooi of the Khoi-Khoi: Under his leadership, and that of Morenga and Maherero, "those brave and talented Herero Chiefs", the united war of liberation of the Khoi-Khoi and Herero tribes (the German authorities had before systematically pitted Khoi-Khoi and Herero against each other) lasted until 1907... In the end the German imperialists with their modern military technique gained the upper hand and staged a cruel showdown, which reduced the Herero population of about 90,000 to a mere 18,000". (Endre Sik).

Herero: They are a people belonging to the Bantu group, with about 120,000 members alive today. The majority of the Herero live in Namibia, with the remainder living in Botswana and Angola. During the 17th and 18th centuries, the Herero migrated to what is today Namibia from the east and established themselves as herdsmen. In the beginning of the 19th century, the Nama from South Africa, who already possessed some firearms, entered the land and were followed, in turn, by white merchants and German missionaries. At first, the Nama began displacing the Herero, but later both peoples entered into a period of cultural exchange. During the late 19th century, the territory became a German colony under the name of German South-West Africa. Soon after, conflicts between the German colonists and the Herero herdsmen began. Controversies frequently arose because of disputes about access to land and water, and also the legal discrimination of the native population by the white immigrants. In 1904, those conflicts resulted in an uprising, known as the Herero Wars, by the Herero and Nama. (Interestingly, the uprising was planned in an exchange of letters among tribal leaders and some of these documents have been preserved). After a period of success for the well-equipped insurgents, the German Empire sent a military expedition corps of about 15,000 men under the command of Lothar von Trotha. The war and the subsequent genocide ordered by von Trotha resulted in the death of between 25,000 and 100,000 (possibly 65,000) Hereros, about 10,000 Nama and 1,749 Germans.

ON THE SOULSCAPE OF THE BULLET TRAIN

Shinkansen: It is a network of high-speed railway lines in Japan operated by Japan Railways. Since the initial T¨kaid¨ Shinkansen opened in 1964, the network has expanded to link most major cities on the islands of Honsh¨ and Ky¨sh¨ with running speeds of up to 300 km/h (186 mph), in an earthquake and typhoon prone environment. Test run speeds have been 443 km/h (275 mph) for conventional rail, and up to 580 km/h (360 mph) for maglev train sets. Shinkansen literally means "New Trunk Line" and hence strictly speaking refers only to the tracks, while the trains themselves are officially referred to as "Super Express"; however, this distinction is rarely made even in Japan. In contrast to older lines, Shinkansen are standard gauge, and use tunnels and viaducts to go through and over obstacles, rather than around them.

Buddha-san: The founder of Buddhism.

Akosombo: See "The Bond Oath of Ubuntu".

Kainji: It is a dam across the Niger River in western Nigeria. The dam is one of the longest dams in the world.

Kalahari: The name of a desert in South Africa.

Kalahari Desert: It is a large arid to semi-arid sandy area in southern Africa extending 900,000 km², covering much of Botswana and parts of Namibia and South Africa, as semi-desert. Derived from the Tswana word Keir, meaning the great thirst, or the tribal word Khalagari or Kalagare (meaning "a waterless place"), the Kalahari has vast areas covered by red-brown sands without any permanent surface water.

A TEA CEREMONY FOR THE NEUTRON BOMB

Yuri Tanimoto: The Japanese girl we encountered during our walk through the garden of a Temple.

Higashiyama Kai'i: (1908-1999) He was a Japanese artist. In 1968 he completed large murals on the New Imperial Palace, and in 1969 he was given the Order of Cultural Merits and designated as a person with cultural merit. In 1975 and in 1980, he completed murals in the Toshodaiji Temple.

Albert Einstein: (1879-1955) He was a German-born theoretical physicist who is widely considered one of the greatest physicists of all time. While best known for the theory of relativity, he was awarded the 1921 Nobel Prize in Physics for his 1905 (Annus Mirabilis) explanation of the photoelectric effect and "for his services to Theoretical Physics". In popular culture, the name "Einstein" has become synonymous with great intelligence and genius. Einstein was named Time magazine's "Man of the Century."

Yukawa: (1907-1981) A scientist who was against the atomic bomb. He and Einstein developed the Atomic Bomb – but after Hiroshima and Nagasaki, started a movement of scientists against the military use of the atomic bomb. In 1955, he joined 10 other leading scientists and intellectuals in signing the Russell-Einstein Manifesto, calling for nuclear disarmament.

Nakpanduri: A town in Northern Ghana.

Alexander Kwapong: Is a Ghanaian academic and classicist, the first African Vice Chancellor of the premier university of Ghana, the University of Ghana, Legon. He was one of the two rectors appointed by U.N. to establish a UN university in Tokyo, Japan. On his return to Ghana he was made Chairman of the Council of State during the Rawlings "Regime".

Humiko Yashima: Our Japanese lady interpreter.

Nara: Is the capital city of Nara Prefecture in the Kansai region of Japan, near Kyoto. Seven temples, shrines and ruins in Nara, collectively form "Historic Monuments of Ancient Nara", a UNESCO World Heritage Site.

Kiyomizu Verandah: To take a great decision is equal to taking a jump down from a Kiyomizu Verandah (the 80 metres high Buddhist Temple in Kyoto).

Himeji Castle: Himeji Castle is famous worldwide as Japan's finest medieval castle and is cherished by the people of Himeji as the symbol of their city. Himeji Castle is also known as Hakurojo (the "White Heron Castle"), because its great castle tower flanked by three lesser towers and elegant white plaster walls create the image of a heron poised for flight. It is said to have originated as a fortress built in 1346.

Nagasaki: It is the capital and the largest city of Nagasaki Prefecture in Japan. It became a major Imperial Japanese Navy base during the First Sino-Japanese War and Russo-Japanese War. Also, the city became the second and last city in the world to be bombed by a nuclear weapon (atomic bomb), following Hiroshima.

Hiroshima: It is the capital of Hiroshima Prefecture, and the largest city in the Ch?goku region of western Honsh?, the largest of Japan's islands. It is known throughout the world as the first city in history subjected to nuclear warfare with the atomic bombings of Hiroshima and Nagasaki in World War II.

Kenzo Tange: (1913-2005) He is a famous Japanese architect, former Professor of the Tokyo University; the (1980) building Tokyo Municipal Office; he was the architect of Imperial Hotel; he did the completely new Imperial Hotel.

DAR ES SALAAM: HAIZEL AT THE 38TH PARALLEL

Pyongyang: The capital of North Korea.

38th Parallel North: It is an imaginary circle of latitude that is 38 degrees north of the Earth's equatorial plane. The 38th parallel north has been, especially important in the recent history of Korea. After the surrender of Japan in 1945, the parallel was established as the boundary between the Soviet (north) and American (south) occupation zones in Korea. The parallel divided the peninsula roughly in the middle. In 1948, the dividing line became the boundary between the newly independent countries of North and South Korea. The 38th Parallel was also the place where the cease-fire was called to end the fighting.

AND NOW TO END THE WORLD NEWS: AGEGEYAN GETHSEMANE

Agege: Is a town on the outskirts of Legos. **Arizona Canyon:** It is in the southwestern part of the United States.

Lord and Chief Justice Apaloo: He was a famous Ghanaian jurist and Chief Justice, noted for his erudition and sound juridical principles. His judgements are often quoted by lawyers. He went away to Kenya, East Africa, where also he distinguished himself as an illustrious jurist. In his final years he returned to Ghana and was honoured by the judges and lawyers.

Masai: The Masai are a very famous warrior tribe in Kenya whose lives center around herding cattle. They live in small settlements of 8-15 huts per kraal. Their settlements are surrounded by a thornbush fence as an added form of protection.

Akwasidae: It is one of the festivals celebrated by the Akans of Ghana.

Gari: It is a preparation from processed cassava used as food.

Nakpanduri: It is a place in Northern Ghana.

Bukom Square: Bukom is an area in Asere, a quarter within the seven divisions (Akutsei) of the Ga Mashie area. Bukom described as a 'city within a city' derived its name from a large well, natural pond – Buko – which served the people in that area as a place for bathing and laundering. To the people of Ga Mashi it used to be the arena for Odododiodoo – an organized free fight match between joint teams of Asere and James Town and Gbese Abola quarters of Accra. This was in the past to encourage and acknowledge the prowess of the youth from various quarters in the city. As an arena for free fights, it is no surprise that Bukom alone bred and produced outstanding boxers like Roy Ankrah, Attuquaye Clottey, Love Allotey, Ike Quartey, Joe Tetteh, Oblitey Komey and others who have put Ghana on the world boxing map. The large well was filled in 1893 by the Government to allow houses to be built hence the coming into being of Bukom Square. It is called Daada Buko: (Daada means: always, eternal). Bukom Square has since become the gathering place of the Ga people.

Nima Highway: It was constructed during the Nkrumah regime. It starts from the King Takie Tawia overpass on Ring Road East, goes through Kanda and Nima and meets the Achimota – 37 Military Hospital road near Gold House and Accra Girls Secondary School.

Krakatoa: (Indonesian name: Krakatau, Portuguese name: Krakatao) is a volcanic island in the Sunda Strait between Java and Sumatra in Indonesia. It has erupted repeatedly, massively and with disastrous consequences throughout recorded history. The best known eruption culminated in a series of massive explosions on August 26-27, 1883. The 1883 eruption ejected more than 25 cubic kilometres of rock, ash, and pumice.

Aflao: It is a border town between Ghana and Togo noted for the immigration activities that take place there.

Gethsemane: It is associated with the crucifixion of Jesus Christ. (also spelled **Gethsemani**) was the garden where, according to the New Testament and Christian traditions, Jesus watched, prayed, and suffered for the sins of the world the night before he was crucified.

According to Luke 22:42-43 (in the Good News Bible), Jesus' anguish in Gethsemane was so excruciating that "his sweat was as it were great drops of blood falling down to the ground." Gethsemane was also where Christ was betrayed by the disciple Judas Iscariot.

Guernica (painting): This is a painting by Pablo Picasso, inspired by Picasso's horror at the Nazi German bombing of Gernika, Spain on April 26, 1937 during the Spanish Civil War. The air raid destroyed the city, killing a number of people variously estimated between 250 and 1,600, and injuring many more. The huge mural was produced under a commission by the Spanish Republican government to decorate the Spanish Pavilion at the Paris International Exposition (the 1937 World's Fair in Paris).

Golgotha: It is another name for Calvary, where Jesus Christ was crucified. Golgotha is said to mean skull.

Sonny Okosun: A famous Nigerian musician. 1977's "Fire in Soweto" really put Okosun on the map internationally.

Okponglo: It is a suburb of Accra not far from Legon on the Accra-Aburi (Dodowa) road.

ABOUT THE AUTHOR

ATUKWEI OKAI was born in Accra, Ghana, in 1941 and was educated at the Gambaga Native Authority School, Nalerigu Middle Boys' School (both in Northern Ghana), Methodist Middle Boys' School (Accra) and the Accra High School, before going to Moscow in 1961, where he earned his M.A. (Litt.) from the Maxim Gorky Literary Institute in 1967. He obtained his Master of Philosophy (M.Phil) degree in 1971 from the School of Slavonic and East European Studies at the University of London, U.K.

In 1968 he was elected Fellow of the Royal Society of Arts (UK); in 1979 he was awarded Honorary Fellowship in Writing of the International Writing Program of the Univeristy of Iowa, Iowa, U.S.A. In 1981 he was elected to Honorary Membership of the National Syndicate of Spanish Writers and to Associate Membership of the Association of Nigerian Authors (ANA). A Fellow and Past President of the Ghana Association of Writers (GAW), he is the Secretary-General of the Pan African Writers' Association (PAWA).

He has taught at the University of Ghana, Legon, since 1971 as lecturer in Russian literature at the Department of Modern Languages and from 1984 till 2001 as Senior Research Fellow in African Literature at the Institute of African Studies. Professor Okai is Head of the GaDangme Education Department at the University of Education, Winneba, Ghana.

Okai's poems have been translated into several languages, including Russian, Spanish, German, Arabic, French, Italian and have appeared in anthologies and several prominent international journals such as The Atlantic Monthly, The New African, African Arts (UCLA), Black World, Literary Cavalcade, The New American Review, and Universitas.

Okai's first collection of poems, **Flowerfall**, was published in June 1969 by Writers Forum in London. His second volume of poems, **The Oath of The Fontomfrom and Other Poems** was published in New York, U.S.A., in June 1971 by Simon and Schuster.

In 1975, the Ghana Publishing Corporation brought out his volume, **Lorgorligi Logarithms and Other Poems** and in 1988, published his book, **The Anthill In The Sea (verses and chants for children).**

Atukwei Okai was awarded the Iqbal Centenary Commemorative Gold Medal by the Government of Pakistan, "in appreciation of valuable contribution to the Birth Centenary Celebrations Seminar on Allama Dr. Mohammed Iqbal, the national poet of Pakistan" in 1979 The International Lotus Prize (and Gold Medal) for Afro-Asian Literature of the Afro-Asian Writers' Association in 1980 acknowledged "the artistic merits of his work."

The C. Marconi Gold Medal of the National Council for Research of Italy in 1986 recognized "his contribution to the International Study Seminar on the New African Literature in Rome".

The **Oath of The Fontomfrom and Other Poems** and **Lorgorligi Logarithms and Other Poems** won The Ghana Book Award of the Ghana Book Development Council in 1979 "in recognition of his signal contribution to the development of national literature".

The **ECRAG FLAGSTAR** award citation in 1991 noted that "You have fought gallantly to place writers on a high pedestal as a driving force behind the Pan African Writers' Association and the Ghana Association of Writers. You have contributed a lot to the study and development of African poetry and African literature in general".

Okai was presented with The Ushio Publication Culture Award of Japan, in 1993. In 1998 the **University of Ghana Golden Jubilee Distinguished Scholarly Award** did "acknowledge his outstanding contribution to the development of African poetry".